ISBN: 978129022701

Published by:
HardPress Publishing
8345 NW 66TH ST #2561
MIAMI FL 33166-2626

Email: info@hardpress.net
Web: http://www.hardpress.net

MEMOIRS

OF THE

CHEVALIER DE JOHNSTONE.

IN THREE VOLUMES.

TRANSLATED FROM THE ORIGINAL FRENCH M.S. OF THE CHEVALIER.

BY

CHARLES WINCHESTER,

ADVOCATE, ABERDEEN.

VOLUME FIRST.

ABERDEEN : D. WYLLIE & SON.
Booksellers to the Queen,
AND H.R.H. THE PRINCE OF WALES
1870

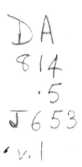
G. CORNWALL AND SONS, PRINTERS AND LITHOGRAPHERS, ABERDEEN.

PREFACE.

The Chevalier de Johnstone, the author of these Memoirs, was successively aide-de-camp to Lord George Murray, created Lieutenant-General of the Forces by Prince Charles Edward, and to the Prince himself, in his abortive attempt to wrest the British Crown from the House of Hanover; and, likewise, a Captain in the army during the stirring period of the Rebellion in Scotland, and thus had the best opportunities of knowing the events which he describes, and discovering the secret springs of action which actuated the minds of those who took part in that disastrous affair.

The Chevalier de Johnstone was the only son of a gentleman of that name in Edinburgh, and his sister, Cecilia Johnstone, was married to John, sixth Lord Rollo, a Scottish Peer of high rank and ancient lineage. His other sister, Jean, was married to John Leslie, Esq., of Crookston, near Dalkeith, the father of Mr. John Leslie, Professor of Greek in King's College, Aberdeen, and the great-grandfather of Hugh Fraser Leslie, Esq., the present respected proprietor of Powis. The Memoirs came into possession of his brother, the late John Leslie of Powis, many years ago, he having acquired

them from Messrs. Longman, Rees, & Co., of London. They
were originally deposited, it is believed, by the Chevalier
himself in the Scots College at Paris, and were seen by the
late Sir James Mackintosh, perhaps the best judge then living,
and by many other literary men of eminence, who all pro-
nounced them the genuine work of the Chevalier, and to
be highly interesting. They came into the hands of
Chevalier Watson, who married the widow of John, sixth
Lord Rollo, and who, for many years, was an outlaw on the
Continent, and from whom they were purchased by Messrs.
Longman & Rees; and they have now been kindly placed at
the disposal of the Editor by his friend Mr. Hugh Fraser
Leslie of Powis.

The Translator is sensible how feebly he has performed his
task, but it has helped to relieve the tedium of a declining old
age, and has afforded him much pleasure and satisfaction in
the translation; and he fondly anticipates that his numerous
kind friends and subscribers will derive no less pleasure from
the perusal.

It is a natural wish of everybody who reads the history of
any great events to know something of the life and manners
of the Historian, and if we have not much to add to the facts
in this case, it will be, at least, satisfactory to know that the
means of information were open and accessible, to afford a
well-grounded hope of their veracity and correctness. Nor
is this all,—we are delighted to follow the narrator through
his trials and difficulties, and see how magnanimously he bore
them, and triumphed.

The opinions of the writer of the Memoirs are interesting and important; and his philosophical reflections give a value to the work which it would not otherwise possess, however much we may differ from these opinions or the conclusions he draws from them.

'The style of the original is simple and consecutive, resembling much that of Cæsar's Commentaries. It gives such a full, clear view, paints the scene in such a vivid manner that you might suppose you saw the whole before your eyes, heard the yells of the Highlanders, and witnessed the clashing of their swords cutting down the English.

It were in vain now to attempt drawing inferences from the failure of the Rebellion; it is an episode in English history that can never be forgotten: and, therefore, it has an abiding influence. Like the siege of Troy, it only wants the lines of Homer to render it immortal. But, apart from its mere interest as a tale of adventures, it holds out many important lessons which history alone can teach—Sweet are the uses of adversity, and great are the uses of history.

Polybius advises his readers to take care to reap profit from its examples, and to apply them to the improvement of life and manners. He says, "There are two sources only " from whence any real benefit can be derived—one, our own " misfortunes, and those which have happened to other men; " for since the first of those, though generally, perhaps, the " most effectual, is far more dangerous and painful than the " other, it will always be the part of prudence to prefer the

" latter, which will alone enable us, at all times, to discern
" whatever is fit and useful, without any hazard or disquiet ;
" and hence appears the genuine excellency of history, which,
" without exposing us to the labour and cost of suffering,
" instructs us how to form our actions upon the truest models,
" and to direct our judgment right to all the different circum-
" stances in life."

One observation may be made,—that the conduct of Lord
George Murray, in disobeying the orders of the Prince to
advance against the English camp at Nairn, on the night after
the birthday of the Duke of Cumberland, was without defence, in a military point of view ; and that the Prince, in
refusing to join his followers at the critical moment of their
rallying at Ruthven, after the battle of Culloden, displayed a
want of courage, and a pusillanimity which proved him to be
totally unfit for the possession of the Crown, which, happily
for his country, he missed. Notwithstanding, his attempt
stirred a national feeling which was creditable to the Scotch,
and must be admired, and is not yet (if it ever can be) eradi-
cated from the hearts of the people. In that respect, history
is like a mirror reflecting the passions and actions of men.
In less than a century what a change has occurred ! The
clans who issued from their romantic glens to do battle for
Charlie, were a peculiar people, a remnant of the ancient
Caledonians, retaining their originality and purity of race,
from having succesfully resisted the attacks of Goths,
Danes, and Norwegians, and even of the Romans, the
conquerors of the world. Indeed, they never failed to be
pleased if they could repel their incursions ; shewing by

their courage in 1745 that it remained unabated by time. Misguided as they were, how fortunate the change!—The Gael being now the brighest jewels in Her Majesty's Crown, and showing, whenever they are called upon, that indomitable courage which marked the career of their ancestors, and has made the Scotch a proud nation.

Perhaps the publication of this volume in the original French MS., side by side with the present translation, might be a desideratum with the learned, as it has never been published in that shape. Indeed, it might be used as a text book, the language being pure, and the style classic.

In the downfall of Troy, our sympathies are with Hector. As the poet puts into the mouth of Jupiter—"They interest me, though they must needs perish;" so with the Stuarts—" With all their faults we love them still."

The second volume of the Memoirs contains an account of the Chevalier's numerous adventures and hair-breadth escapes after the battle of Culloden—first in the deep recesses of the mountains of Scotland, and subsequently in England, till he made his final escape to the Continent in the suite of Lady Jean Douglas, disguised as one of her ladyship's domestics. Then he entered the French service, and was sent as a subaltern to America during the war in Canada. This volume is highly interesting, but as it contains much that is sensational with regard to the Chevalier's attachment to a young lady in London, the daughter of a friend of his family, it is doubted whether the public would be inclined to receive

it with the same approbation as the account of the actual
Rebellion.

The third volume contains notices of the French war
in Canada, in which both General Wolfe and General
Montcalm were killed, on the 13th September, 1759. In a
military point of view, this volume is interesting and important; and it is enriched by sketches of the camps and fields of
battle in that country, as the first volume is of these in Scotland.

NOTICE.

THE popularity of the original Work of the Chevalier de Johnstone may be inferred, from the circumstance of a Translation of the Two First Volumes having gone through Three Editions, in 8vo., the last of which was published in 1822, by Longman & Co., of London. It is now within two years of half-a-century since this last Edition was published; and, although the present Translator does not challenge competition, he can conscientiously affirm that what is now presented to the public is entirely his own; and the value of it is very considerably enhanced by the Chevalier's own original Notes published for the first time, and, also, some added by the Translator himself.

It may be considered rather a bold attempt to undertake a Translalation of what was done so many years ago, and, it maybe, by a far abler hand; but, in answer to this, it may be asked how many translations have been made of Homer, Virgil, and Horace, and Cæsar's Commentaries, but it has never been said that these authors have suffered from these various translations; on the contrary, they have only tended to make their Works better known and more admired. And at the distance of nearly half-a-century, it must be confessed that the previous Translation of a part of the Memoirs of the Chevalier has become very little known, and is now only to be found in the Public Libraries and those of the learned, while the narrations contained in them. as the Editor has already said, have an abiding influence which cannot be forgotten or extinguished. He, therefore, trusts that his numerous Friends and Subscribers will not be disappointed at his having reproduced, and put into their hands a Translation of the First Volume of the Memoirs, containing a relation of the events which, little more than a century ago, attracted the attention of all Europe, and made the King then on the Throne to tremble at what threatened to overturn his dynasty, and left a lesson of thankfulness and humility to the Royal House of Hanover.

ABERDEEN, 11th May, 1870.

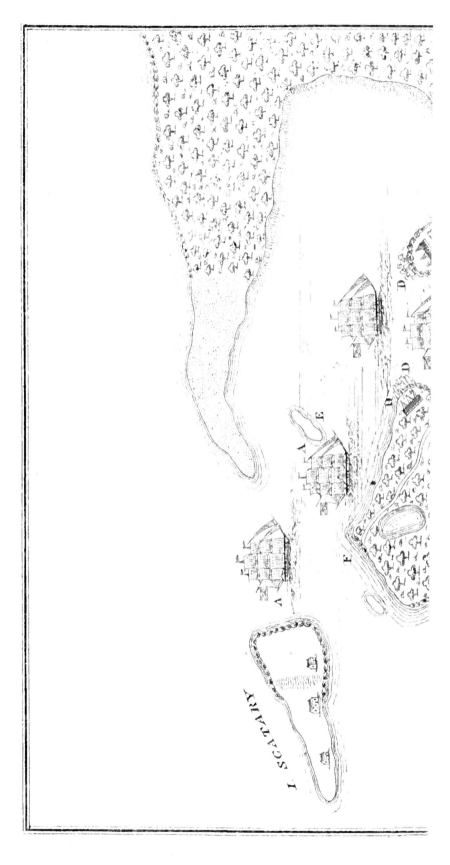

I. SCATARY

SEEMS TO BE THE

LANDING AT

LOCH SOINARD,

ON THE

24TH OF JULY, 1745.

" It is written with a pen of iron and the point of a diamond."

MEMOIRS

OF

THE CHEVALIER DE JOHNSTONE.

Volume First.

CONTAINING AN ACCOUNT OF THE WAR IN SCOTLAND, OR THE
REBELLION OF 1745-1746, IN THE ABORTIVE ATTEMPT
OF PRINCE CHARLES EDWARD TO WREST THE BRITISH
CROWN FROM THE HOUSE OF HANOVER.

PRINCE CHARLES EDWARD STUART,
the grandson of James II., King of England, who
was dethroned in 1688, impatient at the continued
delays in the embarking of troops destined by the
Court of France to make a descent upon Scotland
in his favour, at length formed the resolution of
proceeding there secretly and throwing himself into the arms
of the Scotch. His House had always experienced their
fidelity and attachment since the Revolution, by the different
attempts they had made for re-establishing them on the
throne ; and he hoped to succeed in his enterprise by the sole
efforts of his subjects, without the aid of foreign powers.
He embarked at Belisle, the third day of July, 1745,* in a
small frigate, escorted by the *Elizabeth* a ship of sixty
guns. These two vessels were equipped by M. Welsh, mer-

* In these Memoirs it is always the old style, as was then followed in
England.

chant at Nantes, for transporting the Prince into Scotland. This merchant, in the end, was reimbursed by the Court of France for the whole expense of this armament.

The Prince was not accompanied by more than seven persons : the Duke of Athole, proscribed and in exile since the year 1715; M. Macdonel, an Irishman; M. Kelly, an Irishman, formerly secretary to the Bishop of Rochester, who had been exiled in consequence of a pretended conspiracy of which he had been accused ; M. Sullivan, an Irishman ; M. Sherridan, an Irishman, his old tutor ; M. MacDonald, a Scotchman ; Strickland, an Irishman ; and Michel, an Italian, his valet-de-chambre ;—a retinue sufficiently ridiculous to enter upon an enterprise so bold and audacious as it was, to endeavour to wrest from the House of Hanover the Crown of Great Britain, which it had enjoyed for so long a time : there not being in all this retinue but M. Sullivan alone, who had been in Italy as aide-de-camp to the Mareshal of Maillebois, who had any knowledge of military affairs. The others, Irishmen, attracted into Scotland by the desire of making a fortune, were most injurious to the Prince, and, unfortunately, he bestowed on them his entire confidence.

This Prince after having lost hope of being able to land in Scotland with an army of regular troops, ought at least to have been accompanied by officers distinguished in the art of war by their talents, capable of combining with wisdom and correctness the plans of operations, of conducting them with ability, and who possessed minds fertile in resources, and enlightened by experience, able to discern the momentary advantages that fortune might present, and rapidly to profit by them. With such officers at the head of his army and in his councils, they would have selected for him the place for the disembarkation of the troops, and would have caused him to avoid those errors which in the end produced the ruin of his affairs in Scotland. So much the more as this Prince knew how to gain battles, so much the more did he fail to reap the advantages of which his victories were susceptible.* Besides there was not at that time a general officer in France who would have refused to embark with the Prince in an enterprise so favourable for rendering him in a moment cele- brated throughout all Europe, which had its attention fixed upon this expedition.

It afforded a rare opportunity for displaying talents, which in a numerous army might have perhaps remained always in obscurity and been lost.

The ship *Elizabeth* was attacked in latitude 47 degrees 57 minutes, and 39 leagues west the Lizard point, by the *Lion*, an English vessel of war of 60 guns, of the same force as the *Elizabeth*. They fought for six hours with all the fury and obstinacy possible till both these vessels were equally unman- ageable and ready to sink to the bottom. The combat having ceased, each vessel only sought to keep itself above water and to gain some harbour. The Prince in his little frigate, a spectator of this sanguinary conflict, and so much the more anxious for the event in that he had on board the *Elizabeth* a considerable quantity of arms and munitions of war, caused his frigate approach under the poop of the *Elizabeth* to inform himself of the state of the vessel. They told him that she had lost a great part of her crew, that the captain and many of the other officers were killed, as also many volunteers of Maurepas, who were embarked in her, that the vessel was so crippled by the cannon balls that it was with difficulty she could keep herself from sinking, that she was obliged to make for the first port in France, to repair, which they could reach, not being at all in a condition to continue the voyage. Thus

---

* This was said of Hannibal after the Battle of Cannæ, when his brother Maherbal addressed him in the following language—"Non omnia, nimirum, eidem dii dedere, vincere scis, Annibal, victoria uti nescis."—*Livy, Lib.* xxii. *c.* 51. "Certainly the gods have not bestowed all gifts on the same man. You know how to conquer, Hannibal, but not how to use your victory," when he ought to have proceeded to Rome, and probably secured the empire of the world.—ED.

the two vessels the *Lion* and *Elizabeth*, equally disabled after this combat, mutually retired to their own coasts; and the Prince with his frigate continued his course for Scotland, where he landed the 24th of July, at Loch Soinard, and lodged at the house of M. Macdonald of Kinloch Moidart. He was immediately joined by M. Cameron of Lochiel, with his clan of Camerons, by M. Macdonald of Clanranald, with his clans of Macdonalds, by the Clan of the Stuarts of Appin, and by the other Clans of Macdonalds of Keppoch, Glengarry, and Glencoe. The Macdonalds of Keppoch commenced hostilities on their route to join the Prince, by attacking two companies of the regiment of Royal Scotch, whom they made prisoners, and whom they presented to the Prince as a fortunate beginning.

They did not obtain positive intelligence at Edinburgh of the landing of the Prince until the 8th of August, when they received a messenger from the Chevalier Campbell of Lochnell, with a letter to the Magistrates of that city containing a most circumstantial account of the progress of the Prince since his landing; and this news was speedily spread abroad in public. King George being then in his Electorate of Hanover, the Regent whom he had named for governing the realm in his absence, ordered Sir John Cope, Lieutenant-general of the King's armies, to assemble with all speed the regular forces which were in garrison in Scotland, and to march against Prince Edward without loss of time, with a view to combat and extinguish his enterprise in the bud; and it is greatly to be presumed that this General would have succeeded if he had conducted himself properly; but he lost his advantage by wishing to temporise, (not with the wisdom of a Fabius), though with an army greatly superior in numbers to that with which he had to contend; hoping, perhaps, that by leaving the army of the Highlanders to swell by the continual junction of the partisans of the Prince, he would gain more celebrity by their defeat, and render himself by this means of more importance at the Court of London.

Sir John Cope assembled his army at Stirling, composed of the infantry regiments of Lee, Lascelles, of Murray, of five companies of a highland regiment, two companies of the regiment of Guise, and the dragoon regiments of Gardener and Hamilton. He had six pieces of cannon, and two howitzirs. With this army, and in consequence of orders which he had received from the Regent, he left Stirling the 21st of August, to get before the Prince, but as there are many roads which lead to the north of Scotland, he took that to the east, along the coast. The Prince, on the contrary, knowing positively the route of Sir John Cope, took the road across the mountains by Blair of Athole to descend into the low country—adroitly leaving the English army behind him. Thus, Sir John Cope always pushing his march to the north, and the Prince to the south, it was impossible that these two armies should ever encounter one another.

The Prince arrived on the 5th of September at Perth, a city situated about nine leagues from Edinburgh, where the Highlands, which extend to the west and north-west, commence. He there immediately causes his father, James III., to be proclaimed King of Great Britain—publishing at the same time, the letters patent of his father, dated at Rome, constituting him Regent of the kingdom. At his entry into Perth he had, in all, not more than a thousand men in his train, but the day of his arrival he was joined by the Duke of Perth and his vassals, and by Lord George Murray with a part of the vassals of his brother, the Duke of Athole; also by Lord Nairn, and many other persons of distinction who had attached themselves to his fortune. He sent on the 7th of September a detachment to make the same proclamation at Dundee, which is four leagues from Perth.

When the news of the landing of the Prince was confirmed at Edinburgh, I repaired immediately to the seat of Lord Rollo, a Peer of Scotland, father-in-law of my sister, to await at his house the arrival of the Prince from Perth which is at the distance of a league from his seat; and I left the house of his Lordship the 6th of September, to join the Prince, accompanied by the two Missess Rollo, (who presented me to their parents), the Duke of Perth and Lord George Murray. I was very much surprised on arriving at Perth to find so few people with the Prince, the public report at Edinburgh having exaggerated to an extraordinary degree the number of his followers. Lord George having been created Lieutenant-General by the Prince, with the Duke of Perth to act under his orders; his lordship proposed to make me his aide-de-camp, which I accepted, and I commenced, forthwith upon the spot, to excercise its functions; and the Prince who had only but one, who was M. Maclaughan, employed me likewise, as well as Lord George, so that, night and day, my duties became so multifarious that I had scarcely time to sleep two hours a-day.

The conduct of Sir John Cope was altogether inconceivable, seeing he was regarded in England as an experienced General, and who had greatly distinguished himself in Flanders.

There is an arm of the sea at Leith, the sea-port of Edinburgh, it is two or three leagues broad, but which insensibly narrows itself towards the town of Alloa, about five leagues to the west of Edinburgh, where this arm terminates at the confluence of the river Forth. The Magistrates of Edinburgh had had the precaution to remove from Leith all the Galliots, Barques, Boats, and other crafts, thereby depriving the Prince of all means of being able to cross the Frith. Thus there remained no other manœuvre to be made by Sir John Cope to prevent the Prince from penetrating to the south, but defending the passage of the river Forth, by making intrenchments at the fords, on the side next the town of Stirling, where diverge all the great roads to the highland districts. This town is situated on the Forth, about seven leagues from Edinburgh, and a league and a-half from

Alloa, and half a league from that chain of mountains which extends to the north and north-west of Scotland. There is a stone bridge at Stirling across this river, but it is commanded by the guns of the castle, and Sir John Cope wishing to temporise, could have shut up the Prince in the mountains without another manœuvre. His position at Stirling was very advantageous and centrical, for the purpose of covering Edinburgh, the principal object which Sir John Cope ought never to have lost sight of, since the Prince, above all things, ought to attempt to render himself master of the capital of Scotland, for the purpose of inducing his partizans to declare themselves openly in his favour, by inspiring them with confidence. It is an undoubted axiom, and which should serve as a rule for conducting military operations—"That whatever is for our advantage, is against the enemy ; and whatever is for the enemy's advantage is against us : and that your enemy seeks his advantage with as much eagerness as you can possibly seek yours." So that one can often judge correctly of the enemy's designs by supposing one's self in his position, and considering with himself what he would do in a parallel case—provided the enemy acts according to the principles of the military art, for if the enemy's general is an ignoramus, a Marshal Turenne would be as much embarrassed to divine his intentions, as anyone who had never learned to make arms his study, would embarrass the most skilled.

General Cope by shutting up the Prince in the mountains would have prevented him from making a coup d'etat, so essential at the commencement of his expedition to the success of his enterprise ; and the Prince would have never attempted to pass this river with a strong force at the mouths of the fords intrenched, and bristling with cannon. Besides, the Prince would have gained but little in stealing the passage of this river by ascending towards its source, where he would have been obliged to go up the country district of the Campbells, a clan of Highlanders, numerous, and implacable enemics to the House of Stuart, of which the Duke of Argyle is the chief. But above all, General Cope had his two regiments of Dragoons to scour this part of the country by his advanced posts and patrols, till within three or four leagues of his camp at Stirling. And supposing that the Prince had passed this river, Sir John Cope could have then advanced to give him battle under all possible advantages, preserving always his position between the Prince and Edinburgh. In case the army of the Prince had advanced to the Fords, as it would have certainly done, General Cope had nothing better to do than, when the Prince was sufficiently close not to be able to escape him, but to pass the river by the bridge at Stirling with his army, and fall upon him unexpectedly upon the mountains while the Prince would be attempting the Fords. The issue of the combat could not have been doubtful,—Sir John Cope having three or four thousand men of regular troops in his army, against from twelve to fifteen hundred undisciplined Highlanders. But there was then from thirty to forty leagues distance between the two armies ; and Sir John Cope—whether it was by his ignorance in the art of war, notwithstanding the reputation he had gained, (which one sees is often ill founded) —or whether it was by cunning or evil intentions against the good of the service, in place of crushing the Prince at his outset, he allowed an enterprise to become strong, the astonishing and rapid progress of which surprised and fixed the attention of all the Potentates of Europe; and he was himself the victim of his own ignorance, or cunning, as ordinarily happens. Thus, the Prince with a small number of miserable highlanders, shook the throne of Great Britain, and was within an ace of being crowned at London. He maintained himself against the whole united forces of England, who were further augmented by Hessian and Dutch troops ; and he gained many battles against armies of regular troops greatly superior in number to his own. This is perhaps an event unparalleled in history, and which posterity will hardly believe.

The Prince left Perth the 11th September, and on the 13th he crossed the Forth at the Ford of Renfrew, four miles above Stirling. On the 14th, in the evening, our army arrived before Corstorphine, a village about half a league from Edinburgh, and passed the night in a field at Gray's Mill, where the Prince lodged in the cottage of the miller. There came there during that time deputies from Edinburgh to treat respecting capitulation. The Prince answered them that he would not treat with his subjects. They were in the meantime immediately on good terms; and next day, in the morning, the Prince was conducted to Holyrood-house, the Palace of his ancestors, in the suburbs of Edinburgh, amid the acclamations of an immense multitude of people, whom curiosity had drawn out to meet him, about a quarter of a league from the city. This was a novelty, the Scotch having been deprived of the presence of their Kings since the Revolution; and they even have come but very seldom since the union of the two crowns under James I., the son of Mary Stuart, at the death of Queen Elizabeth.* The next day King James was proclaimed at Edinburgh, and Prince Edward nominated Regent to govern in the absence of the King his Father, who was at Rome.

General Cope arrived on the 11th of September at Aberdeen, a town at about thirty leagues north of Edinburgh, and having decided to embark his army to return to the south by sea, he ordered transport ships to come hither, and having had a favourable wind, he landed on the 17th with his army at Dunbar, a town about six leagues east of Edinburgh, where he was immediately joined by two other regiments of dragoons lately arrived from England, with brigadier Fawkes, who commanded them, also by the Dragoon regiments of Hamilton and Gardiner, whom he had left at Stirling on departing for the north of Scotland.

* That cannot be said now, since our beloved Queen has a palace at Balmoral in Aberdeenshire, where she spends about a fourth part of the year, making excursions through the Highlands, and occasionally in other parts of her Scottish dominions, "None making her afraid."—ED.

Lord George Murray who had charge of the whole detail of our army, and who conducted it entirely, had a natural genius for war, and surprising talents, which, cultivated by the study of the military art, had rendered him truly one of the greatest generals of Europe. He was tall, robust, and brave to a high degree, conducting heroically the Highlanders, always at their head, always the first to dash in the midst of the enemy, sword in hand. He used to say when he led them to the charge, "My boys, I don't ask you to advance before me, but only to follow me," a speech truly animating for exciting the ardour of the Highlanders, but which would sometimes have been better applied in the mouth of the Prince. He was indefatigable, sleeping little, occupied continually with all the details, and he combined and directed alone all the operations; in fact he alone was capable of conducting our army. His colleague, the Duke of Perth, although brave even to intrepidity, a perfectly upright man, endowed with a great deal of sweetness of character, was of a feeble genius, and intermeddled with nothing. Lord George was vigilant, active, and diligent. The execution of his plans was prompt, and his combinations always correct.* Notwithstanding, with an infinity of great qualities, he was not without his faults. Fierce, haughty, blunt, and proud, he desired always to dictate everything by himself, and knowing none his equal, he did not wish to receive their advice. It is true that there were few persons in our army sufficiently instructed in the military art to be in a condition to give him any for the direction of his operations. The Chiefs of the Highlanders, like their vassals, were of a heroic bravery, but they knew no other manœuvre than to rush upon the enemy sword in hand as soon as they came in sight of them, without order and without discipline. His Lordship could still less derive any enlighten-

---

* One would say of Lord George Murray what Robertson says of Charles V., "he joined to a profound sagacity in the combination of his plans great constancy and firmness in the execution of them."—Vol. ii., page 307.

ment from the Irish subaltern officers, who, with the exception of M. Sullivan, were instructed in the simple knowledge of subalterns, which consists generally in knowing how to mount and relieve guard. It is not then astonishing that Lord George, endowed with all the qualities requisite for making a great General, should have gained the hearts of the Highlanders (and a General having the confidence of his soldiers can do miracles); also possessing the art of availing himself usefully of the services of men without having time to discipline them, and such as they were on quitting the plough. He made them perform incredible prodigies against different English armies of regular troops, always infinitely superior in numbers to those of the Prince, who, in the meantime, were known as being the best troops in Europe. Nature had formed him for being a great warrior by himself without the aid of fortune.*

* Suntse, a Chinese general, gives all the particulars necessary for making a great general, of which the greater part might be applied to Lord George Murray. " Be," says he, "vigilant and open, but showing outwardly a great deal of security or simplicity, and even indifference ; be always on your guard, although you should appear to be thinking of nothing ; defy all though you should appear without defiance ; be extremely secret, although it should appear that you have nothing to discover ; have spies everywhere, in the very palaces of the prince, your enemy, in the hotels of his ministers, under the tents of his generals. The more you disperse your spies the more you gain—it is a bribe to obtain a great interest. You ought to suppose that the enemy will also have his own spies. If you come to discover them, to be careful to put them to death. Their days ought to be to you infinitely precious. The enemy's spies you deceive effectually if you direct your marches, your patrols, and all your actions in such a manner that they can never give out a false impression to those who have sent them to you. See with your mouth, speak with your eyes. Punish severely, reward liberally. Have justice and discrimination in distributing seasonably your punishments and rewards. Love your troops, and provide them in all the succour, all the advantages, and all the requisites of which they could possibly stand in need. If they undergo severe fatigues, it is not that they are pleased with such. If they endure hunger, it is not that they are regardless of what they may have to eat. If they are exposed to death, it is not that they do not love life. Husband your corn with discretion. Those who are properly instructed in the art military make all

The Prince caused a corps of Highlanders to enter Edinburgh, which formed immediately a blockade of the castle, where there was a garrison of from five to six hundred men, in order to prevent sallies, and deprive it of the means of annoying us in the city. . In the meantime he caused the rest of his force to be encamped at Duddingston, a village at a quarter of a league from his palace at Holyrood-house.

Sir John Cope encamped at Haddington, about four

their marches without disadvantage, all their movements without disorder, all their attacks by a stroke upon their defences without surprise ; their encampments with special choice, their retreats by system and by method. They must know their own forces ; they must know whatever they may be those of the enemy ; they must be well acquainted with whatever concerns localities. A skilful general makes of himself alone more than all his army. He knows how to discern and appreciate a good action whatever it may be ; to distinguish between faults which one may commit, those which might produce results from those that are of no consequence ; and to repair opportunely both the one and the other ; to possess an undoubted firmness when it is employed in causing discipline to be observed ; to choose and instruct, without any exception, those who ought to be employed. Shut up all those of your own soldiers you see deserting, and open, on the contrary, the gates and facilitate the entry of the soldiers of the enemy ; receive with kindness all those of the opposite side, and make them subservient to your interests by the intelligence of those who are in a condition to give good counsels ; and have the art of penetrating their true sentiments, when even by whatever motive of fear, policy, or interest they dare not declare them openly. Favour industry and all military talents ; reward bravery, punish laziness, excite emulation, and stifle murmurs ; make every one move according to his wish, and when one wishes it, that is to have authority established. It is necessary to gain the hearts to secure the esteem and conciliate a well-grounded fear. It is necessary to be just, impartial, fully straightforward, and disinterested, by means of which he will destroy every subject of discontent or murmuring, and make himself beloved even when inflicting punishments and chastisements. A general ought to be magnanimous, he ought to be prudent, he will be bold without rashness, fierce without presumption, firm without obstinacy, exact without pettishness, attentive without distrust, circumspect without suspicion. He ought to be clear and precise in all the orders he gives, constant to exact them, exact and inflexible in causing them to be executed. He should never have ill humour, never caprice, never a view to his own interests, but always affable, always kind, full of that tenderness that nobody can call in question or be in doubt about."

leagues east of Edinburgh, the 19th of September, and on the 20th he approached to within a league and a half of our camp. As it was absolutely indispensable in our situation to give battle, the rather that the greater part of the partisans of the Prince only waited the event of a combat to declare themselves and join his army, the Prince assembled his whole force on the morning of the 20th of September, and began his march at once to get before the enemy. The army of the Prince was composed of about eighteen hundred men badly armed, part of them had only sticks in their hands. There were found very few arms in the city of Edinburgh, the inhabitants, before surrendering, had sent their arms to the castle, which is very strong on account of its situation, being on the top of a rugged rock, and impregnable on account of its height, except by bombs or by famine. The army of General Cope was composed of about four thousand men of regular troops, besides some volunteers which fanatical zeal had inspired to join themselves to him, but who had not sufficient courage to be hurtful to us. We arrived, towards two o'clock in the afternoon, within musket shot of the enemy's army, where we stopped behind an eminence, (f.) having a full view of the camp of Sir John Cope, the position of which was chosen with all possible skill. The more we examined it the more we saw the impossibility of attacking it, and every one stood aghast, not knowing what course to take. On equal ground the courage and bravery of the Highlanders might make up for want of numbers, but what could be done with eighteen hundred men against four thousand in a position inaccessible on all sides. The camp of the enemy was fortified by nature, and this was a singular position for so small an army as his. This general had on his right two enclosures (c. c.) surrounded by stone walls from six to seven feet high, between which there was a road of about twenty feet broad which led to the village of Prestonpans. Before him he had another enclosure (d.) surrounded by a deep ditch and full

of water, from ten to twelve feet broad, which served to set
the marshy ground afloat. On his left he had a morass which
terminated in a pond, the water in which was deep ; and he
had behind him the sea which shut him up as in a fortification,
unassailable otherwise than by a siege. We proceeded after
mid-day to reconnoitre his position, and our anxiety and
chagrin tended only to augment at every moment by our dis-
coveries of the locality, seeing no means of attacking him
without visibly exposing ourselves to be hewn in pieces with
dishonour.

At sunset our army crossed the village of Tranent, which
was on our right, taking up a new position *(g.)* opposite the
morass. General Cope at the sametime placed his army in
four divisions, supporting his right against the ditch of the
enclosure, *(d.)* his left to the sea, and having his front to the
pond. Mr. Henderson, the proprietor of the morass, came to
the Prince about night-fall, very opportunely to relieve us
of a terrible embarrassment. He assured the Prince that
there was a passage through the morass where we could pass,
and that he had crossed it daily in shooting. The Prince
having sent at once to reconnoitre the passage, found his report
correct, and that General Cope, believing it impracticable, had
neglected to place a guard on it. During the night he made
his army to pass over it. The Highlanders defiling one after
another without encountering any opposition on the part of
the enemy, formed their ranks according as they got out
from the morass, and the column extended itself along the
seashore.

General Cope at daybreak mistook for bushes our first
line, which was in battle array, about two hundred paces in
front of his army. It consisted of about twelve hundred
men, and our second line of six hundred was composed of
those who were badly armed, many as we have said above,
having only sticks in their hands. Mr. Macgregor, Captain
in the regiment of the Duke of Perth, in default of other

arms, took scythes, well sharpened, which he attached to the ends of sticks from seven to eight feet long, the points in height like the lance of a spontoon, with which he armed his company, and which, was a most murderous weapon.

When the first line had passed the morass, Lord George Murray sent me to watch for the purpose of seeing that the second line, which the Prince conducted himself, should also pass it without noise or confusion. Having surveyed the spot, and not finding anything in disorder, in returning to rejoin Lord George, I found the Prince at the head of this column with Lord Nairn; at the moment he entered the morass, and that I had crossed it with him for the second time, we were not again beyond it when the enemy fired his alarm gun on perceiving at the break of day our first line in battle array.

Close to the edge, on leaving the morass, there was a deep ditch, three or four feet broad, which it was necessary to leap, and the Prince in jumping it, fell on his knees on the other side, and I seized him by the arms immediately, and raised him up. On examining his countenance, he appeared to me to be struck by this accident as an evil omen.

Lord George, at the head of the first line, did not leave the English any time to recover from their surprise. He advanced at quick time and so precipitately, that General Cope could with difficulty put his army in battle array; and the Highlanders threw themselves upon them, head foremost, sword in hand. They had been often recommended to deal their sword strokes upon the noses of the horses without attacking the horsemen, explaining to them that the natural movement of the wounded horse in front, would be to make him bolt round; and that a few wounded horses at the head would be sufficient to throw a whole squadron into disorder, and without their being able to remedy it. They followed this advice with exactitude, and the English cavalry were immediately in disorder.

The Macgregor company with their pikes made most dreadful carnage. They cut in two the legs of the horses, as well as the horsemen through the middle of the body. Macgregor was very brave and intrepid, but at the sametime, altogether wild and eccentric. In advancing to the charge with his company, he received five wounds, two of which were from musket balls, which pierced through his body from side to side. Resting extended on the earth, his head on his hand, he called out to the Highlanders of his company—" My lads, I am not dead, by G——d, I will see if every one does not do his duty." The Highlanders fell at the instant on the flanks of the English infantry, who being broken and exposed by the flight of the cavalry, yielded immediately. Thus in less than five minutes we gained the most complete victory, with a frightful carnage on the side of the enemy. It was obtained with such rapidity, that in the second line where I was always beside the Prince, not having been able to rejoin Lord George, we saw no other enemy upon the field of battle, but those who were upon the ground killed or wounded, although we were not but fifty paces in arrear of our first line, always using our legs as fast as we could to join them, and sufficiently near to them never to lose sight of them; even being able to distinguish them always before us through the smoke from the discharge of the enemy, the only time we had to see them. The Highlanders made a slaughter of the English principally at the entry of the road between the two enclosures, which was immediately blocked up by the fugitives; as also along the walls of the enclosures, where they killed without difficulty those who were clambering up to enter them. The strength of their camp proved their destruction. Some of them rallied at first in the enclosures (e. e.) where there was an eminence which commanded the field of battle, and from which they fired some shots of musketry; but they were immediately dispersed by the Highlanders who entered after them into the same enclosure.

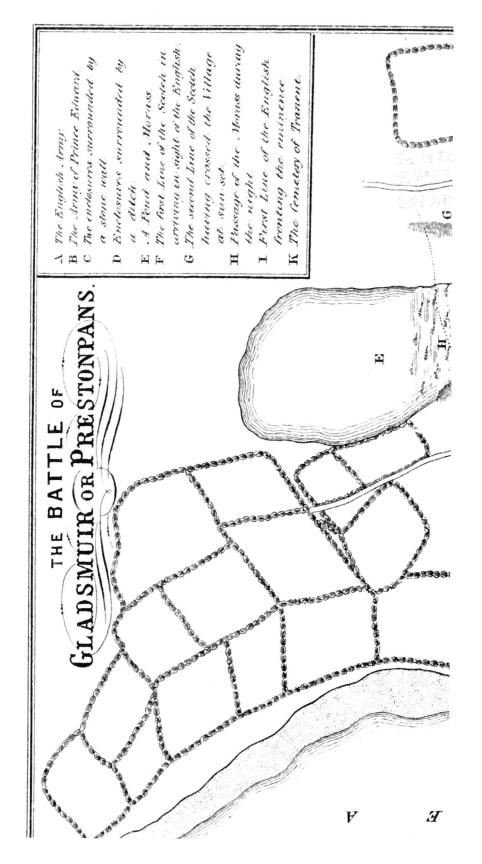

THE BATTLE OF
GLADSMUIR OR PRESTONPANS.

A The English Army.
B The Army of Prince Edward.
C The enclosures surrounded by
   a stone wall
D Enclosures surrounded by
   a ditch
E A Pond and Morass.
F The first Line of the Scotch in
   arriving in sight of the English.
G The second Line of the Scotch
   having crossed the Village
   at sun set.
H Passage of the Morass during
   the night
I First Line of the English
   fronting the eminence
K The Cemetery of Tranent.

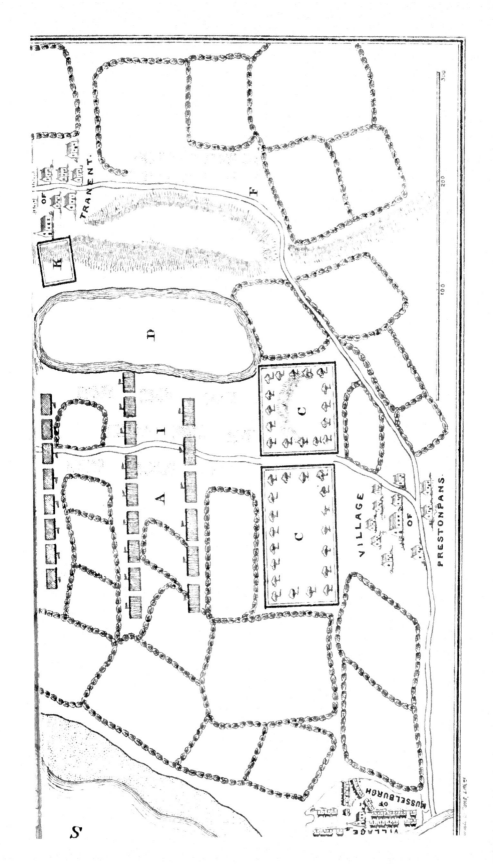

The field of battle was a spectacle of horrors, strewed with arms, legs, heads, and mutilated corpses, the whole having been slain by sword strokes. The enemy had thirteen hundred men killed; we made fifteen hundred prisoners, and we took six pieces of cannon, two howitzers, all their tents, baggage, and military chest. General Cope, by means of a white cockade which he had placed on his head, like to those which we wore, passed through the midst of the Highlanders without being recognized, and saved himself in England, carrying thither himself the news of his defeat. This victory lost us but forty men killed, with about as many wounded.* But the greatest advantage which we reaped from it was the reputation which it brought to the arms of the Prince at his first outset, which determined a great many of his partisans who were still vacillating to declare openly in his favour. The arms of the vanquished, of which we stood much in need, were also of great service. This battle was fought on the 21st of September, O. S. The Prince passed the night at Pinkie House, about a quarter of a league from the field of battle. He charged me with the care of a hundred and ten English officers, our prisoners, with orders to watch them, and see that they should want for nothing.

The panic terror of the English surpasses imagination,— they threw down their arms upon the ground to enable them to fly more quickly, thus depriving themselves, through fear, of what might have arrested the vengeance of the Highlanders disposed to punish them. Of so many men in a condition by their number to make head against us, not a single one dared to dream of defending himself, terror had

* We see examples of this without number. The Romans lost in the battle of Cannæ 50,000 men, (according to Polybius, who is an accurate historian, 70,000); and Hannibal lost only 700. At the battle of Platæa, according to Herodotus, of 300,000 men of which the army of Persia was composed, only 40,000 escaped with Artabazes, who took to flight, and 3,000 others; and the Greeks lost only 91 Lacedemonians, 16 Tegeates, and 52 Athenians, in all 159.

so taken possession of all their minds. In a situation to have preserved themselves by their courage, they did not dream but of saving themselves, every one separately by flight. Fear always deprives people of reason. I saw a young Highlander about fourteen years of age, and who was not yet formed, whom some one presented to the Prince as a prodigy for having slain fourteen English soldiers. The Prince asked him if that was true. The young man replied "that he did not know that he had killed them, but he had knocked down fourteen soldiers with a stroke of his sword." I saw another Highlander who brought to the Prince ten English soldiers, whom he had himself alone made prisoners, driving them before him like a flock of sheep. This Highlander, with a boldness without example, having gone after this troop alone to some distance from the field of battle by the road between the two enclosures *(c. c.)* felled to the ground the hindermost of them with a stroke of his sabre, calling out at the same time "Down arms." These affrighted soldiers immediately threw down their arms without looking behind them, and the Highlander with a pistol in one hand and his sword in the other made them manœuvre at his pleasure. One can imagine the rage and despair of these soldiers at seeing themselves made prisoners by a single man. These, however, were the same English soldiers who had been at Dettingen and Fontenoy, and who could be reckoned with justice among the best troops in Europe. Above all, it is not astonishing that these Highlanders, who had taken up arms voluntarily from attachment to their legitimate Prince and their Chiefs, should throw into disorder triple the number of regular troops whose soldiers are enlisted by seduction or licentiousness. They have not the same love of glory, affection for their Prince, the sacredness of patriotism, the profound sentiment of a just war, the hope of rich spoils, or an honourable promotion. It is the command of a Prince who forms and augments armies, and orders them to march as it seems good to him.

Having many times seen routs since this battle, I have always remarked that the loss of soldiers which we sustained was much less in the battle than in the pursuits. Seized with dismal terror in their flight, and often dragged along with their comrades without knowing the cause, and with less loss in men than the enemy who remains victorious, they disperse themselves like sheep, beyond the power of being able to defend themselves, and present themselves as if victims to be slaughtered. Thus it did not require an extraordinary degree of courage in that young man to kill fourteen men; but it was a feat rather bolder to brandish fourteen strokes of the sabre over the heads of those men who fled, and good legs to be able to run as fast as they, and to catch them. The other Highlander who made these ten soldiers prisoners might have paid for his rashness and temerity if they had had the presence of mind to look behind them when he cried out, "Down arms." Can they not be impressed with the spirit of soldiers when their safety and existence even depend upon their temerity—their *sang froid*—when the only means. of making themselves respected by a victorious enemy, and saving themselves from the carnage that always follows a defeat, or to join themselves to their comrades as soon as the disorder begins to show itself, and to rally themselves by forming a corps as quickly as possible? When in retiring with precipitation, by a retreat like that of Diomede, the head always turned to look at the enemy, the success of battles would not be so considerable as it ordinarily is—at least the carnage which generally follows it would not take place.* The

* "Every warrior," says Outse, the Chinese General, "ought to regard the field of battle as the place where he should finish his days—if he seeks to live he will perish; on the contrary, if he fears not to die, his life is in safety." This is the same reflection as that of Xenophon. "They who the most endeavour to preserve their life," says Xenophon, in his *Retreat of the Ten Thousand*, "are not those who live most carefully, but those who, knowing that death comes to all men, seek to render themselves glorious, and often arrive at an honourable old age." It is, after all, the educa-

victorious enemy would not dare to break the order of battle to follow, for fear of exposing themselves, to see their victory snatched from them without enjoying it, as has happened more than once. It is ever deemed prudent that a victorious army should advance slowly, and preserve itself in order as much as is possible, leaving a bridge of gold to his enemy in flight! and it is generally only the light troops and the cavalry that are employed in the pursuit. The sight of a corps

tion that we give to man, and the manner of training him, which moulds him to be what we should wish him to be ; for, as Hobbes observes, "reason is not born with us, as are the senses and memory, and it is not acquired by experience alone, as prudence, but by industry," &c. J. J. Bourlamaqui says, in his *Treatise on the Principles of Natural Laws*, "Let us figure to ourselves a man become full grown without having had any education, or any commerce with other men, and consequently without any other knowledge than what he would acquire for himself, he would be, beyond contradiction, the most miserable of animals, and would see nothing in himself but weakness, ignorance, and barbarity ; with difficulty would he be able to satisfy his bodily wants, and he would always be ready to perish of hunger or cold, or by the teeth of some ferocious beast." The Abbe Condillac goes still farther—" Every one," says he "who has been deprived of all commerce with men, and who, with sound organs, and properly constituted, would, for example, be elevated among bears. He would be almost without recollection, and pass often through the same state without remembering that he had been in it. Without memory he would have no power to supply the absence of objects. Having only an imagination which he could not make use of, his perceptions would not awaken, except when chance presented an object with which some circumstances might have connected it. In fine, without reflection he would receive impressions which things would make upon his senses, and he would not obey them but by instinct. He would imitate brutes entirely ; would utter a cry nearly resembling theirs, and drag himself along on his feet and hands. We are so very prone to imitation, that perhaps a Descartes in his place would not attempt alone to walk upon his feet." *Origin of Human Sciences*, p. 178— "I do not advance," continues he, "these but as mere conjectures. In the forests which separate Lithuania from Russia, they caught, in 1694, a young man about ten years of age, who lived among the wild beasts. He gave not the slightest signs of reason, walked on his hands and feet, had no language. He uttered sounds which resembled nothing like those of a man. As soon as he was able to speak they interrogated him about his former state, but he remembered nothing more than that which we remember to have happened to us in the cradle." *Idem*, p. 202—" Behold the primitive state of

retiring in order imposes upon them. " He who pursues his
enemy in disorder," says Machiavel. " will lose the victory
which he has gained, and perhaps give it to the enemy."
The rallying of troops always appeared to me one of the most
essential things in the military art; but to arrive at that point
of perfection in discipline, it is necessary to have made man's
study; to know his inmost sentiments, the different characters
in particular, and in what they unite, is generally a profound

man without one first instruction, and without having the least intercourse
with men. By education in his youth we can give him what impressions we
please. On his entering into troops it is a second education, under an
authority despotic and severe as our military ordinances, and we can mould
him, like clay, to whatever we wish." "But a philosopher," says Robertson, "contents himself with observing that the character of nations depends
on the state of society under which they live, and the political institutions
established among them; and in all times and in all places men placed under
the same circumstances would have the same manners, and exhibit themselves under the same forms." *History of Charles V.* vol. ii. p. 34 — " It is
only the youth that enlist into corps who are not yet free from the preju-
dices of their earlier education and capable of being drilled according to
the ideas of good sergeants, who are the soul of companies, the same as old
lieutenant-colonels and commandants of battalions and regiments; and this
same principle in individuals forms them altogether the same. One can drill
soldiers to whatever one may wish."—CHEV^L^R.

If it were not irrelevant here, we might quote the opinion of Montesquieu upon the subject of education in general, which is worth treasuring
up. He says, " The laws of education are the first impressions we receive."
He farther observes, " The principal branch of education is not taught in
colleges or academies. It in some measure commences when we enter the
world, for this is the school of which we all hear, the universal preceptor,
which ought everywhere to be our guide. Hence it is that we constantly
see and hear three things—that we should have a certain nobleness in our
virtue; a sort of frankness in our morals; and a particular politeness in our
behaviour." He well adds —" Men born for society are born to please one
another, and a person that would break through the rules of society by
indecency would lose the public esteem, and in so far become incapable of
doing good. Politeness," he says, " arises from the desire of distinguishing
ourselves. It is pride that renders us polite; we feel a pleasing vanity in
being remarked for a behaviour that shows in some measure that we are
not meanly born, and that we have not been bred up with those who in all
ages have been considered as the lowest of the people."—ED.

and difficult science, but essentially necessary for the General of an army, who in commanding men despotically ought to know of what they are capable. To impress the minds of soldiers with the necessity of rallying promptly, as soon as they fall into disorder, and to retire slowly before the enemy, presenting their arms to defend themselves, it is not necessary to point out to them that on this depends the safety of their life, in view of the certainty of losing it by being dispersed in flight without being in a condition of defence. As every man, by his nature, cares for his own preservation, the soldier, convinced that in joining himself to his fellow-soldiers to form battalions he can secure his life, and oppose himself with advantage against a smaller number of the enemy employed in the pursuit, he should so conduct himself; and this is means more efficacious than all the orders and threatenings that the officers can employ. It is not in the idea of losing their life which makes them give themselves over to flight, but in the view of preserving it, and being more out of danger. They deceive themselves only in the means, and precipitate themselves to death in place of avoiding it. Soldiers are machines, to drive which one ought to direct and impede, that they might not be governed despotically by the imagination. I have seen them advance to the attack like lions; repulsed, one would not know them to be the same men, becoming in an instant powerless and fearful as hares. In the meantime, it is not the diminution of their number in the shock which has been able to effect this sudden change, for it is impossible for them to know what is passing in the distant parts of the army; but they turn their backs mechanically, without having any other reason to give but the example of those that are beside them. The contagion communicates itself throughout the whole army with the rapidity of lightning. An unexpected resistance on the part of the enemy deranges the whole order of the machine, and reverses in an instant the power of reflection and discernment, and they see nothing but trouble. It is of the nature of man in general to be inconstant and variable, rarely distinguishing objects with correctness, and by consequence with no stability in his opinions, and almost never in accord with himself.* Hence it is necessary to raise the imagination of soldiers, which is the only director of their actions; and the confidence with which a general is able to inspire his army of his capacity, talents, and experience, is the best key which he can avail himself of. Soldiers securely in the favour of their general comport themselves like heroes, believing that they are marching to certain victory; and with troops animated as the Highlanders were at this singular battle, a general ought not to regard the number of his army, although far inferior to that of the enemy, but to the disposition of the spirits of his soldiers. It is certain that an army composed of the same men may be despicable when commanded by such a general, whereas it shall be invincible when commanded by such another.

The next day, the 22d of September, the Prince returned to Edinburgh with his army, and he was there received with the greatest acclamations of the people, always equally inconstant in all parts of the world. He there issued many of his proclamations, of which he had one in which he made an excuse for having rejoicings on account of his victory over the army of General Cope, seeing that it had not been obtained but by the effusion of the blood of his subjects; and another which granted a general amnesty for all treasons, rebellions, and offences committed against him or against his predecessors

---

* More or less contrary to himself by reason of his tastes and fancies, weakness renders him timid, experience of evil timorous, and ignorance credulous and foolish, in his terrors. Such is man on all the face of the earth. It is not climate that makes them what they are. It is *opinion*, which is itself nothing more than a collection of ideas transmitted and perpetuated by education, religion, government, and continually fortified by example and habits, which serve to identify them, so to speak, with ourselves.

since the Revolution in 1688, provided the offenders' delivered themselves up at his palace of Holyrood-house within the space of four days, and that they there made a declaration before his Secretary that they would live in future under his dominion as quiet and peaceable subjects. He sent at the same time circular letters to the Magistrates of all the towns of Scotland, commanding them immediately to repair to Edinburgh in order to pay their contingent of contributions which he had imposed upon each town; he also caused despatch other letters to the collectors and comptrollers of customs throughout the land, as well as to those of the revenue, ordering them to bring with them to his Palace their registers and the money arising from the taxes which might happen to be in their hands, under pain of the crime of Lease-Majesty.

This victory, little important as it may appear at first sight, rendered, nevertheless, the Prince entirely master of the kingdom of Scotland, where there remained no more English troops, except the garrisons in the castles of Stirling and Edinburgh, all the towns of Scotland having been obliged to acknowledge the Prince under the title of Regent of the Kingdom, as governing the same during the absence of his father, King James, who was then residing at Rome. He did not presume in the meantime but to maintain possession of it. It behoved him to have for his principal object to find out all the means possible for confirming himself in the government of his ancient kingdom of Scotland, and to maintain it against the English armies which would undoubtedly be sent against him, without by nowise extending for the present his views upon England before he was perfectly well established and in a condition to face their invasions. This was the general advice that everybody gave the Prince, and if he had followed it, perhaps he would have been still in possession of the kingdom. They advised him strongly to set aside and annul at once the Act of Union of Scotland with England, as having been made during the usurpation of Queen Anne by a cabal of some peers of Parliament of Scotland whom the English had allured to their interests by force of money, and contrary to the general voice of the Scottish nation, who, even to the last peasant of them, always held that Act in abhorrence. This measure would have been infinitely pleasing to all Scotland, and the sole consideration of being freed from the English yoke would have been sufficient to engage the Scotch in general to declare in his favour. In fomenting also the natural hatred and animosity which the Scotch have manifested on all occasions against the English, the war would have become national, and this was all that the Prince could hope to make it fortunate. The Scotch, though greatly inferior in numbers to the English, had, nevertheless, always borne up against them during a long war, almost continually of a thousand years, and had preserved their liberty and independence even to the Union of the two kingdoms in 1707. Above all, the Prince being able to establish himself in Scotland, the Court of France would feel its interest to maintain him on the throne, and would employ all their forces to prevent his reunion with England. They adduced in the counsels which they gave the Prince, that in consequence of the annulment of the Union, as an act made during the usurpation, and prejudicial to his Royal House, it was necessary to expedite the writs for convoking at once a Scottish Parliament at Edinburgh, in order to impose the taxes in a regular manner, and to have supplies to be able to keep together and subsist his army. It is true that this parliament not being composed at first but by the partisans of the Prince, could not be regarded as a free parliament; but the sums imposed upon the nation in this manner would appear less arbitrary, and would carry along with them more an impress of justice and legality on their form than the military contributions of which he availed himself. There were those of Scotland, the most distinguished by their superiority of genius, good sense, spirit, and judgment, who pointed out to the Prince this plan of

C

wise, sensible, and salutary operation, but which he did not appear to relish, having inherited entirely the sentiments of his ancestors, who had always had an absurd predeliction and affection for the English nation, and had always been victims of the blind attachment with which that House had governed them in place of conducting them with a rod of iron as their predecessors, Henry VIII. and Queen Elizabeth, had done. The Prince rejected constantly every proposition which could lead to displease them or give them the least umbrage. This unfortunate House of Stuart, always abhorred and detested by the English nation from their accession to that crown, had never received any return for their tender sentiments for the English, but only persecutions, even to the extent of making their blood flow upon the scaffold, and finishing by chasing out of England the whole race, and despoiling them of their crown. The Prince, in the meantime, had his mind occupied only by England, and appeared little flattered by the possession of the kingdom to which, nevertheless, the race of the Stuarts owed their birth and royalty.

The army of the Prince, since this victory, increased every day, and amounted, immediately, to from four to five thousand men. Then he was seized with impatience to march into England, and for that purpose he assembled a council of all the Chiefs of Clans that he might act alone by their advice. King George being returned to London since the 11th September, and alarmed at the defeat of General Cope, he caused recall to England all the English troops which were in the allied armies in Flanders. On representing to the Prince the ridiculousness of attempting to make an invasion of England with so small a force to oppose itself against fifty thousand regular troops, without counting on an enormous militia, some of the Chiefs said to him that it was to make him King of Scotland that they had taken up arms in exposing themselves to perish on the scaffold, with confiscation of their goods, but that they had nothing to do with England. In the meantime the Prince pretended to have received letters from many English lords, assuring him that he would find them on the frontiers of England, under arms, ready to join him with a considerable corps of English; the Chiefs of the Clans allowed themselves to be brought about, and consented, in the end, to his proposition, after much debate. Thus the Prince, in place of remaining in Scotland on the defensive, left Edinburgh with his army the 1st of November, where he scarcely had sojourned a sufficient length of time to discover whether he was entirely master of his kingdom of Scotland, and what arrangements and just measures it would be necessary for him to adopt for preserving the conquest of it. The enterprise was bold, rash, and without example! How could he venture to confront the English armies, and attempt the conquest of England with four thousand five hundred Highlanders? It is true they were brave, resolute, and determined to fight to the last in selling their lives, and having no middle course to choose, but to conquer or die. But the disproportion was monstrous,— this number being opposed to the whole united force of England.

The army of the Prince staid in the town of Dalkeith, about a league and a-half from Edinburgh, till the 3rd of November, when it took the route for England. But before our departure, two vessels, one a Spanish, and the other a French, having landed fortunately at the harbour of Montrose on the 11th of October, laden with money, arms, ammunition, and six field pieces of Swedish manufacture, with a detachment of French gunners, their cargoes arrived at Dalkeith. There arrived, at the same time, many Irish officers in the service of France, of whom M. Grant, an eminent mathematician, who had wrought during a long time with M. Cassine, in the observatory at Paris, was of the number; also M. D'Aiguille, brother of the Marquis of Argout, who took the title of Ambassador of the King of France.

The disposition of our march was very well ordered, and

very well executed ; similar, in a small degree, to that which M. the Marshal Saxe made in the grand one some years after, to form the siege of Maestrich. There are three great roads which conduct from Edinburgh to London ; one which follows the east coast of Scotland to enter England by the town of Berwick-upon-Tweed, and which passes by that to the city of Newcastle-upon-Tyne; this is that which is commonly taken; another by the west coast of Scotland, where it enters England at the city of Carlisle, of old the border place of the English against the incursions of the Scotch, as was the town of Berwick at the other side of England; and the third in the centre, between the two others. Our army formed itself into three columns, and each column took one of the roads in departing from Dalkeith, so as to hold, by these feints, the English in doubt of the true direction, by which the Prince intended to penetrate into England. This manœuvre had so well succeeded that Marshal Wade, newly landed in England, waited us at Newcastle-upon-Tyne, with eleven thousand men, which he had withdrawn from Flanders, comprising therein a corps of Swiss troops in the pay of England; and he remained always in the same position, to cover and protect from insult that city, which is one of the most considerable in England. This was a secret so well guarded, as befits military operations, that scarcely any person in our army had the least idea of the spot where our three columns were to unite again ; and we were all very much surprised, in finding ourselves all at once re-assembled on the 9th of November, almost at the same instant, upon a waste heathery common in England, distant about a quarter of a league from Carlisle—this march having been combined with such correctness, and executed with such precision, that there were not two hours of interval in the arrival of the three columns.

Carlisle, a considerable town of England, is not distant from the borders of Scotland more than a league and a-half.

The river Esk, which is fordable, and about half as broad as the Seine at Paris, forms the boundary between the two kingdoms in this part, as the river Tweed does on the side of Berwick. The fortifications are ancient, and entirely neglected since many ages, that the long wars between Scotland and England have ceased, and since the peace confirmed by the union of the two Crowns at the death of Queen Elizabeth. It is surrounded by walls, which are flanked by towers with ditches; and it has a citadel, where they have a great deal of artillery, with a garrison of invalids. This citadel was at one time very considerable, but presently its walls, as well as those of the city, are falling into decay. We opened the trenches before this place, under the orders of the Duke of Perth, on the night of the 10th or 11th of November, about 40 *toises* from the walls—M. Grant, an Irish officer of the regiment of Lally, who executed in our army the functions of engineer-in-chief, having availed himself ably of the ditches of the enclosures, which conducted us so close to the town under cover from the fire of the enemy. Our artillery was composed of these six pieces of cannon from the Swedish foundry, which arrived from France with M. Grant, and the six other field pieces, of a lesser calibre, which we had captured at the battle of Gladsmuir (Prestonpans).

The Prince being apprized that Marshal Wade was in march with a view to compel us to raise the siege of Carlisle, and that he was already advanced with his army as far as the town of Hexham, as it was very important to give him battle before penetrating into England, in order to preserve our communication with Scotland, he departed with his army to get before him, leaving the Duke of Perth with a small force to continue the siege of Carlisle; but the Prince having rested some days at Brampton, a small town about eight miles from Carlisle, and about as many from Hexham, to await him, upon the positive information that the army of Wade had departed from Hexham to return to Newcastle, he came back with our army to Carlisle, and had the pleasure during his route to receive the keys of that city from deputies who had come to meet him to capitulate. It surrendered the third day after the trenches were opened, more by our threats to fire red-hot balls, and to reduce the town to ashes, than by the force of our artillery, not having fired a single cannon shot, for fear of letting the enemy know the smallness of their calibre, which might have encouraged them to defend themselves. The town at first wished to surrender without the citadel, but the Prince having refused to receive the one without the other, the terrified inhabitants forced the citadel to surrender along with them, and the garrison was made prisoners of war. The soldiers, after having given their parole of honour not to carry arms again against the House of Stuart for a year, were sent back. It is inconceivable how Marshal Wade, known by every one as the most able general officer in the service of England, had not advanced on Brampton to fight the Prince and arrest his progress, having an army of regular troops more than double the number of that of the Prince; whether he feared to expose himself openly against the Highlanders after the recent example of the disgrace of his brother officer, Lieutenant-General Cope, who had thereby so dishonoured himself, or whether on account of the maladies which reigned in his army, his soldiers not being accustomed to the fatigues of a winter campaign; whether he, following the orders and particular instructions of King George to hazard nothing, and not to depart at any distance from Newcastle, fearing lest the miners, who were there to the number of twenty thousand, might seize this favourable opportunity to revolt and join the Prince, in order to free themselves and their posterity from their perpetual slavery in the coal mines, he remained always in inaction under the walls of that city.

M. Patullo, our Commissary-General, made a review of our army at Carlisle, and it amounted to four thousand five hundred men. The Prince then held a council composed of all the Chiefs of the Clans, at which he pretended to have again received new letters of assurance from his English partizans, whom he would find all at Preston with arms in their hands. The Chiefs strongly represented to him the danger of attempting to penetrate so far into England with such a small force; and that the best course to be taken was to return to Scotland, to fix his residence at Edinburgh, waiting until he were in a condition to change it into an offensive one, and there carry on a defensive war, seeing, above all, that the succours which he hoped for from the English by their promises of joining him on the Borders had vanished into air. The Prince insisted always on advancing into England, and the Chiefs at length consented thereto.

Our cavalry left Carlisle the 20th of November, to remain all night at Penrith, a town of England about a dozen of miles from that. It consisted of two companies of guards of a corps composed of young gentlemen, of whom Lord Elcho, at that time Earl of Wemyss, and a Peer of Scotland, a nobleman equally distinguished by his birth as by his rare merits, commanded the first company; Lord Balmerino commanded the other. There was another corps of guards, a company of a hundred and fifty gentlemen on horseback, commanded by Lord Pitsligo.

On the 21st the Prince left Carlisle with the infantry, and slept at night at Penrith; and Lord Elcho with the cavalry which he commanded as first captain of the corps of guards, passed the night at Shap, a village eight miles to the south of Penrith. The Prince on departing from Carlisle left a garrison of from two to three hundred men in the citadel. On the 22d the cavalry advanced as far as Kendal, and the army with the Prince sojourned at Penrith. On the 23rd the army came to Kendal. On the 24th the cavalry passed the night at Lancaster, and the infantry reposed itself at Kendal. On the 25th the cavalry advanced as far as Preston, and the infantry passed the night at Lancaster.

On the 26th the cavalry, having passed the night at Preston, occupied a village near the suburbs of that city, and our infantry advanced to Preston. The Prince there held a council of the Chiefs of Clans where he gave them to hope anew of the junction of his English partizans on his arrival at Manchester, and induced the Chiefs to continue to advance into England. The whole army sojourned there the 27th to repose itself.

On the 28th our army left Preston, and passed the night at Wigan, and on the 29th at Manchester, where it sojourned till the 30th.

On the evening of the battle of Gladsmuir (Prestonpans), the Prince having given me the commission of Captain of infantry, without being attached to any regiment, wearied of the functions of aide-de-camp to Lord George, which knocked me up with fatigue, I applied myself forthwith with diligence to raise a company, and when it was complete attached it to the regiment of the Duke of Perth, shaking myself clear of this distressing employment, but this was not done without calling forth a little bad humour on the part of Lord George, who did not wish that I should leave him. M. the Duke of Perth attached me immediately to the artillery with three other companies of his regiment, a charge almost as painful as that which I had just left, having been obliged often to pass the nights on the highways exposed to the blue empyrean, and without shelter in the midst of winter, in weather the most severe, when some carriage was broken in pieces by the bad roads, in guarding the artillery, in waiting till the artificers should have them repaired.

One of my sergeants, named Dickson, whom I had engaged from among the prisoners which we 'made at Gladsmuir (Prestonpans), a young Scotchman, brave and intrepid as a lion, and much attached to my interests, came to render me an account at Preston on the 27th, that he had beat up all the journey for recruits without finding any, and he was so much the more chagrined that the other sergeants were much more successful. He asked of me, at the same time, permission to go before the army a day's march, in proceeding at once to Manchester, a very considerable town of England, where there are forty thousand inhabitants, in order to be able to strike a blow before the arrival of the army. I scolded him much on account of his extravagant proposition in venturing to expose himself by this rash march to the risk of being taken and hanged, and I ordered him to go back again to his company. Having great confidence in him I had given him a horse, and he carried my portmanteau behind him, to have it always with me. On entering my lodgings to go to bed, my hostess told me that my sergeant had come to take my portmanteau and blunderbuss. I perceived, immediately, his rashness, and his conduct annoyed me much; but the next day, on the evening of the 28th, on my arrival with the army at Manchester, Dickson presented himself before me with about a hundred and eighty men, whom he had enrolled for my company. He had left Preston in the evening with my kitchen apparatus and his mattress, and, having marched all night, he arrived next morning at Manchester, which is twenty miles from Preston, where he had commenced immediately to beat up for recruits. The populace, at first, did not disturb him, believing that our army was approaching the city; but from its being made known that it could not arrive till towards the evening, then they assembled tumultously around them with an intention of making them prisoners or killing them. Dickson having the blunderbuss charged with a handful of blank shot lowered it to his cheek, threatening to kill the first of those who should dare to approach him, and turning continually upon his heels to present face everywhere, comporting himself as a lion, he cleared, immediately, a circle which an immense crowd of people had formed around him; having continued this manœuvre for some time, those people of Manchester who were attached to the House of Stuart took up arms and rushed on to Dickson, to save him from the fury of the people, in so much that he had presently five to six hundred men to his assistance, who immediately dispersed the crowd. Then Dickson, triumphant, and placing himself boldly at the head of this escort, paraded quietly the whole way down the streets with the drum, enlisting for my company all who offered themselves. Moreover, on giving me the muster rolls of these one hundred and eighty recruits, I was, further, agreeably surprised at finding by the account of the expenses that they had not cost me, on the whole, more than about from two to three guineas. This adventure of Dickson's occasioned a good deal of pleasantry, by the city of Manchester finding itself ludicrously taken by one sergeant, one drum, and one girl. One may judge from this trait that the bravery of our army amounted even to fanaticism ; and that the panic-struck terror with which the English were seized was inconceivable. I did not profit by these recruits, to the great regret of Dickson. M. Townly, an old officer in the service of France, having joined the Prince some days before, obtained a commission as Colonel, with permission to raise a regiment composed entirely of English ; and the Prince ordered me to pass over to him all those whom Dickson had enlisted for me. It was called the Manchester Regiment, and never exceeded three hundred men, of which the recruits of my sergeant made up more than the half. This was all of the English that declared themselves openly for the Prince, so that the Chiefs of the Clans were not much in the wrong in not trusting to these pretended succours, which the Prince believed infallible.

On the 1st of December the army left Manchester, and passed the night at Macclesfield ; on the 2nd the cavalry took up their position at Congleton, a town about three leagues from Newcastle-under-Lyne, where was the army of the Duke of Cumberland, composed of about six thousand men of regular troops, and who retired immediately to Lichfield, at the approach of our cavalry. Lord Elcho having suddenly pushed himself forward to Newcastle-under-Lyne, to reconnoitre the enemy, there took prisoner M. Weir, chief spy of the Duke of Cumberland. On the 3rd, our cavalry went to Ashbury, having passed by Leeds, where our infantry stopped to pass the night. On the 4th our army reached Derby, a pretty considerable city, about thirty leagues from London, with about fifty thousand inhabitants.

The army of the Duke of Cumberland not being above the distance of a league from Derby, our army passed all the day of the 5th in that city, occupied in preparations to give battle the next day in the morning. There was a very great disproportion in the numbers of the two armies, but the inequality was made up by the heroic ardour of the Highlanders, animated this special day to an inconceivable pitch, and breathing only to be led to the combat. They were seen all throughout the march, collecting in crowds before the cutlers' shops, who were quarrelling among themselves who should be the first to whet and give an edge to their sabres. This fire and ardent desire for engaging in battle, might well compensate for inferiority in number. While all these preparations were going on to give battle to the Duke of Cumberland the next morning, there arrived at Derby a courier from Lord John Drummond, brother of the Duke of Perth, and the despatches with which he was charged, changed entirely the face of our affairs. Lord John informed the Prince of his landing at Montrose in Scotland, with his regiment of Royal Scots, raised lately in France, and with some picquets of the Irish brigade; he added in his letter to the Prince, that before his departure from France, all the Irish brigade was embarked, besides many French regiments; and that he had made all the speed possible that they should arrive in Scotland, before even his letter should reach him. He informed the Prince at the sametime, that he had three thousand men along with him, as well as these troops which he had left in

France, and by the Highlanders who had not been able to join him before his departure for England. On arriving at Derby, they had sent a courier to London, who returned the next day, and reported that besides the army of the Duke of Cumberland, which was within two or three miles of Derby, they had further another army of thirty thousand men, which waited for us at Finchley Common; the greater part of which, however, with the exception of the regiments of Guards, consisted only of militia. After mid-day of the 5th the Prince held a council on the despatches with which these two couriers were charged, which lasted a long time, and in which the debates were very animated. The question for deliberation being, if they should continue to advance to London, or if they should retreat to Scotland to avail themselves of the reinforcement of the three thousand men, who were with Lord John Drummond, and wait in Scotland the succours from France, of which Lord John had announced the arrival without delay. The Prince was strong in his advice to give battle the next day in the morning of the 6th of December, to the army of the Duke of Cumberland, and proceed on to London; but he was the only one of this opinion. The Chiefs of the Clans, since the council held at Preston, had not contradicted the Prince in anything that he had proposed; seeing themselves too far advanced into England to retreat, engaged in the extravagant enterprise, they felt that they had no other part to choose but to continue their adventure, and conquer or perish, sword in hand;—for if defeated in England, not a soul in our army would ever be able to save himself; not only the English peasants being bitter against us, but there was still the army of Marshal Wade in our rear, to cut off our communication with Scotland. This news of Lord John changed entirely the prospect and state of our affairs, in announcing that there were three thousand men with him, and the succours of the Court of France which could, according to the plan which Lord John had directed, be landed in Scotland, and already on the march to join us on the frontiers of England. The Chiefs of the Clans then represented to the Prince, that with such dispositions as we perceived in our army, we could not doubt but that we should easily vanquish the army of the Duke of Cumberland, although greatly superior in number to ours; but that we could not hope for victory without its costing us more or less of our force; and an army also small as ours, of four thousand five hundred men, against the whole united force of England, could not afford to suffer the least diminution. Above all, having another battle to give, immediately against the other English army at Finchley Common, before that we could reach London; that supposing by a miracle in our favour, we should arrive even at the gates of that capital without losing a man, what kind of figure could four thousand five hundred men cut in making an impression on a city of more than a million and a-half* of inhabitants,—adding especially, that the Prince ought to see clearly with regard to his English partizans, that in place of having procured throughout all the counties of England any who were reputed to be attached to his House, in order to facilitate their junction, he had not found a single person of distinction who had desired to declare himself. The Duke of Perth alone, at first took no part in the debates between the Prince and the Clans, leaning his head on the mantle-piece, and hearing the dispute without saying anything; but at the end he was loudly in the opinion of all the other Chiefs. The Prince always persisted obstinately on going to London. He maintained that they would run more risk of being all cut up in retreating into Scotland than in marching onward,—seeing that the Duke of Cumberland the moment that he knew of our retreat would not fail to pursue us hotly, and keep himself always at our heels; while General Wade, who had certainly orders to put

---

* What a difference of population at this day, when the city of London is said to number nearly three millions of inhabitants.

himself with his army between us and Carlisle, would block up the road to Scotland, in so much that we should find ourselves infallibly by this manœuvre on the part of the enemy, between two fires, and that we should all be enclosed as in a net.

The Chiefs of the Clans replied to the Prince that our army being without the encumbrance of baggage, and the Highlanders very nimble and indefatigable, of which they had given so many proofs since they came into England by marches of twenty miles a-day without leaving stragglers behind, having only some hours in advance on the army of the Duke of Cumberland, it was impossible that he could ever overtake us. His army could with difficulty make twelve miles in a day of winter in bad roads without leaving behind the half of his soldiers, therefore we could not have that army upon our hands. As to that of Marshal Wade, we also had little reason to fear it, since we had entered England; that on the contrary it was to be wished for us to encounter it to beat it; we should depart gloriously out of England sword in hand. This it was what would console the Highlanders for the failure of their hopes by their retreat.

In short, the retreat was determined upon for the next morning, the 6th of December, and in order to conceal it we left Derby some hours before it was day. The Highlanders, believing at first that they were in march forward to attack the army of the Duke of Cumberland, testified great joy and alacrity; but as soon as the day began to clear in the distance, and that they perceived we were retracing our steps, we heard nothing but howlings, groans, and lamentations throughout the whole army to such a degree as if they had suffered a defeat. They heard in London on the 5th of December of our arrival at Derby, and the next day, which the English call Shrove Monday, this news immediately published through the whole city caused there a terror and consternation inconceivable to all the inhabitants, the greater part of whom retired to the country with whatsoever effects they deemed most precious, and all the merchants shut their shops. Every one ran to the bank for payment of their notes, and bankruptcy was only avoided by a stratagem. It did not refuse payment of the notes; but it was just that those that arrived first should be the first to be paid, and they were careful to have constantly their officers posted with their notes who surrounded the counter, and they paid them in small pieces to consume the time in counting them. These gentlemen departed by one door with the money which they had come to receive, and returned by another, in so much, that those who had notes could never approach the counter to be paid, and the bank following this method saved its credit, and even kept countenance with its creditors. Having learnt, at the sametime, that our army was only within the distance of a league from that of the Duke of Cumberland, they looked every moment for the news of a battle, of which they tremblingly anticipated the issue, and expected to see our army, in two or three days, enter London in triumph. King George made all his yachts come with speed to the quay at the tower, causing them to embark on board all that he had most precious, and ordered them to hold themselves in readiness to depart at a moment's notice. They assured me in London, when I was there after this occurence, that the Duke of Newcastle, Minister and Secretary of State for War, kept himself shut up in his house the whole day of the 6th. deliberating upon the course he should take. and in uncertainty if he should not declare himself all at once for the Prince. They even pretended at London that there were fifty thousand men collected in that city to go out to meet the Prince. and join themselves to his army; and nobody in that capital actually doubted that if we had beaten the army of the Duke of Cumberland. we should not have found another English army at Finchley Common, which would have even dispersed of themselves; and that in advancing immediately to London. we would have taken possession of that city without finding there the least opposition on the part of the inhabitants, nor the shot of a gun on the part of the troops. The King having taken the resolution of embarking without delay, in case the issue of the battle at Derby, with his son the Duke of Cumberland, should not prove favourable, and to set sail immediately for Holland,—thus we should have seen, without comprehending it, a revolution take place in England, equally surprising and glorious for the small number of Scots who had accomplished it, and which posterity could scarcely believe. It is true that the English were quite ignorant of the number of our army by the care we took in all our marches to conceal it ; and it was next to impossible that their spies could have ever been able to discover it—we not arriving in the cities till night-fall, and departing in the mornings before day. In all the English Gazettes, they always made the number of our army to amount to twelve thousand or thirteen thousand men.

I dare not decide if we were well or ill founded in retreating to Scotland. It is only the Supreme Being who is able to penetrate into futurity, amid the darkness which conceals it from mortals, and who can forsee obscure and unexpected events, which often overturn suddenly the best combined and the most profound projects of the greatest men. The human mind is too limited in its foresight on the subject of accidents. It can only judge by appearances, and form its decisions as to consequences which might naturally flow from them.

Continuing always to advance and confront the whole troops of England, united with that of the Hessians and the Swiss, the appearances in regard to us were that we should be quickly annihilated and cut to pieces, without a single man of our army escaping. Bravery, amounting to ferocity, could not do impossibilities, and must of necessity yield to numbers. It is in the analysis of projects that we ought to search for the proof of their solidity, and find the truth—not in the event.

As Prince Eugene was in want of resources in his surprise of Cremona, and obliged to retire after having been the whole day in possession of that city, nevertheless, the justness of the combination in his plan of operations, and his sagacity in the execution of them, became for ever the admiration of military men, and justified him to himself; having succeeded according to all human probabilities, which is all that can be required of a General. In forming his plan he could not have foreseen that after he should have entered the city without being discovered, and been in possession of all the posts and public places, an unfortunate guide—whom he had sent to conduct a detachment to a bridge to make himself master of it, in order to let Prince Rupert, who was on the other side of the river with a body of troops, enter the city,—should mistake the streets which conduct directly thither; and that he should lose by this mischance half-an-hour's time, in the precious moments which he chose to conceal his project. He could no more foresee the obstinate and unheard of defence of a garrison whose General had been made prisoner, and in which there did not remain a single superior officer to command and direct its manœuvres, every plain subaltern commanding-in-chief his own little platoon, composed of soldiers of different regiments, who joined themselves together with those whom even they met by chance coming out of their lurking p'aces. But if Prince Eugene had undertaken to engage with four thousand men to fight to-day an army of ten thousand, and to-morrow another army of thirty thousand, and to take possession, immediately after that, of a city of a million and a-half of inhabitants, what would sensible men have said of his project? There was not the slightest appearance of fifty thousand issuing out of London to join our army, since, throughout all our progress, we had always seen the English very ill disposed towards us, except at Manchester, where there appeared some scintilla of attachment to the House of Stuart: but when we were certain of this reinforcement at

London, it might probably happen before it could be in our power to join them, to pass under the bellies of these two armies, and still not having to give battle, for the English people talked much but did not like blows, nor to go far from their own firesides. Besides, supposing even that we had beaten the army of the Duke of Cumberland on plain ground, the debris of his army would have rallied on Finchley Common and reinforced this army.

If Lord John Drummond, at his landing, had advanced by forced marches, as he ought to have done, to join us on the frontier of England with his three thousand men, in place of remaining in Scotland in inaction, certainly no one of our army would have ever given his opinion for a retreat, with such assurances as we had of these succours from France; and it is very certain that if Lord John had not landed in Scotland, we were engaged so deep in this adventure in England, with no prospect of having anything better to do than to continue it, we would have all been captured as brave men, or we would have been in possession of London and King George dethroned; there would have been no other alternative in it. Lord John was still more inexcusable in sending the Prince the false information of these succours of ten thousand men from France, which he believed so true from the positive assurances in his letter to count upon them, that every one in our army imagined them to be already landed in Scotland. On marching in the mornings, the first thing we did was to look at the wind if it was favourable, and at every instant we expected news of them. This false report of Lord John Drummond greatly influenced us in making us adopt the resolution at Derby of retiring into Scotland.

The 6th of December the army of the Prince passed the night at Ashbury; the 7th at Leeds; the 8th at Macclesfield; the 9th at Manchester; the 10th at Wigan, and the 11th at Preston, where it remained the 12th; the 13th it arrived at Lancaster, where it remained the 14th to rest; the 15th it arrived at Kendal, where we were then assured, by certain information, that we had left the army of Marshal Wade behind us, and that there was more than risk that it would be able to cut off our communication with Scotland. Lord George Murray, always informed of all that passed in the hostile armies, knowing often even by their emissaries the movements which they premeditated making, had this advantage considerably over those who were ignorant of all that regarded our army, and had no knowledge of anything that passed there.* In order to be more particularly informed of the position of the army of Marshal Wade, which was very close to us at Kendal, having quitted that which he occupied so long a time at Newcastle-upon-Tyne under orders from the Duke of Cumberland, to post himself between us and Scotland to cut off our communication, as he had intended at Derby, but by some hours only of delay in his march we had the start of him, Lord George took a detachment of body-guards to reconnoitre for himself the position of the English army, with which he got out at twilight, and returned in two hours with several English whom he had made prisoners, who gave him clearly the precise information he went in search of.

The Prince having taken a fanciful taste for battles from the ease with which he had gained the victory at Gladsmuir or Prestonpans, with small loss, he was always inclined to fight, not sparing at times even reproaches to Lord George for his unwillingness to expose himself to the events of a

---

* Epaminondas used to say that there was no talent so useful to a General as that of being able to find out the resolutions and designs of the enemy, and to discover by conjecture that which he could not ascertain by certain information.

Lord George (Murray) did still more—he even took every part in making all his operations with so much secrecy that the army of the Prince had continually their ears deceived and their eyes fascinated ; nobody ever knew where we were going, nor what we were going to do, till the moment of its execution. If his own people were ignorant of the designs of the General, how could his enemies be able to discover them ?

battle, when he could derive no advantage from a victory, and for having hindered him from fighting the Duke of Cumberland at Derby. Lord George said to him one morning at Kendal, at the moment that our army was putting itself in order to march—"Since you are always for battles at all risks, I offer you a battle in three hours hence against the army of Wade, which is at the distance of not more than three miles from us, which I have ascertained myself this night." The Prince answered him nothing, mounting immediately into his vehicle; and the army put itself in motion at once to continue our retreat.

On the 16th our army passed the night at Shap, and our artillery stopped at a league and a-half from Kendal. Some carriages of ammunition having broken down at that place, we were obliged to pass the whole night upon the highway, through frightful weather of wind and rain. On the 17th the Prince, with the army, arrived at Penrith; but the artillery, with Lord George and the regiment of MacDonalds of Glengary, of five hundred men, which remained with us to reinforce the ordinary escort, could only reach Shap, and, moreover, with great difficulty, at nightfall. On the 18th, at break of day, we left Shap with the artillery to rejoin our army, which stopped at Penrith to wait for us, but we were not far on the march till we espied many light horse of the enemy, who galloped incessantly around us, without in the meantime daring to approach us within musket shot. The appearance of these light horse seemed the more extraordinary as until then we had not seen any of them since our entry into England. Having arrived at mid-day at the foot of an eminence, which it was necessary to cross to get to Penrith, about half way from that town to Shap, the instant we wished to ascend it there appeared a whole troop of cavalry, marching two and two, upon the top of the heights, who disappeared immediately, as if to form themselves in battle array behind the eminence, which concealed from us their number, with the design of disputing the passage. We perceived at the same time a prodigious number of trumpeters and kettle drums. M. Brown, colonel in command of the regiment of Lolly, was at the head of the column, with two companies of those which the Duke of Perth had attached to the artillery, of which mine was of the number; after them followed the cannon and the carriages; at the last, two other companies attached to the artillery. Lord George was in front of the column. We stopped a moment at the foot of the eminence, every one supposing that this was the English army from the great number of kettle drums and trumpets, and in this desperate case we were immediately, by the advice of M. Brown, to fall down headlong upon them, and dash through them sword in hand, in order to join our army at Penrith or to perish in the attempt, having no other course to choose. So without apprizing Lord George of our resolution, we rushed forward with velocity, mounting the eminence, running as fast as our legs could carry us. Lord George in the rear, seeing our manœuvre at the head of the column, and not being able to pass the carriages in the deep roads bordering the hedges, where we then were, caused the Highlanders pass across an enclosure to attack the eminence on another side, they ran so fast that they reached the summit of the eminence almost as soon as those who were at the head of the column. We were agreeably surprised, having mounted to the top, on finding that in place of the English army, this was nothing but three hundred light horse and chasseurs, who betook themselves to flight in disorder, without our being able to overtake but one single man, who had been thrown from his horse, and whom we wished to make prisoner for the purpose of obtaining some information from him; but it was impossible to divest him of the fear of the Highlanders, who cut him in pieces in an instant. According to appearances, from the prodigious number of trumpeters and kettle drummers which these light horsemen had, it was their design to turn us from the road to Penrith by making us believe that the whole English army was before us upon the height; and if we had fallen into the trap which they had set for us, there was not a single man of our detachment that in two hours time could have escaped being killed or made prisoner.

We resumed at once our march, but in less than an hour, a carriage with ammunition having broken down by the bad roads, we were óbliged to stop our course. The singular adventure of these light horsemen had made me uneasy, not being able to comprehend their effrontery, at least that the army of Marshal Wade was not so far from us as we imagined it to be. I imparted my conjectures to M. Grant, who commanded the artillery, and at the same time that he was our engineer, an officer of great talents, and I proposed to him to accompany me to a farm which we saw about half a quarter of a league from us upon our right, to endeavour to find a carriage there, in order not to lose the time that would be necessarily consumed in repairing that which was broken down. He consented to it, and we took with us seven or eight men, of which my Sergeant Dickson was one of the number. Having found a carriage in the court-yard of the farmer, we seized it on the spot, and our march was no farther delayed than the time necessary to remove the ammunition from the broken-down carriage and to put it on the other. In returning from the farm Dickson wished us to observe something which appeared to us black-like upon the top of an eminence, at the distance of about a league from us on our left, and he maintained alone, against every one else, that he saw it moving, and that it was the English army, adding that it was bearing down upon us. As no one but himself could distinguish anything, taking that which he saw for bushes, I treated him as a visionary; but he persisted always that it was troops; and I made him hold his peace, telling him that it was fear which conjured up an army in his imagination; meanwhile, to have the last word, he replied that we would see in an hour whether he was right or wrong.

Having advanced about two miles, we became immediately convinced that Dickson had better eyes than ours. The Duke of Cumberland having followed us by forced marches with two thousand cavalry troops, as well as foot soldiers mounted, his cavalry fell most unexpectedly upon the MacDonalds at the rear of the column with all the fury and impetuosity possible. Fortunately, the road being bordered with thorn hedges and ditches, the cavalry could not deploy to surround us, nor make a greater front than the breadth of the road, to be able to attack us on every side. The Highlanders sustained the check with heroic firmness; thrust them back with blows from their sabres, and did not budge out of their place until the artillery and the carriages were distant from them a hundred paces, continuing their route; then the Highlanders wheeled half round to the right and rejoined the carriages, running with all their might; as soon as they came up to them they stopped again, firm as a wall, to receive the cavalry which charged them at a brisk trot as before, and were repulsed in the same manner with slashes of their swords. In short, we marched about a mile, the cavalry charged continually without intermission, and were as often repulsed, the Highlanders always repeating the same manœuvre, and comporting themselves like lions.

At Penrith, the Prince being apprized but imperfectly of our adventure with the light cavalry, put his army under arms, and departed immediately from that city to be before us, and the English cavalry having escorted us in this manner till quite opposite Clifton Hall, *(g.)* which is at the distance of half a league from Penrith, the sight of our army in order of battle made them slack their pace. This cavalry then entered the enclosures of the castle which were surrounded by hedge-rows, where the horsemen alighted on the ground, and formed themselves in order of battle in the enclosures, presenting front to our army, which was upon a moorland, the hedges of which separated the two armies, which were not distant from each other more than a small musket shot.

M. Cameron of Lochiel being at the head of our army
with his vassals, having passed the bridge after the first position *(d.)* of our army, to escort us and succour us, was the
first to join himself to Lord George Murray with his regiment
of Camerons, and to protect Lord George with the regiment
of MacDonalds of Glengary from the English army. The
sun was just on the point of setting when our detachment
joined the army. The Highlanders approached the enclosures
where the English were. They went down upon their knees
to the ground to cut with their dirks the thorn hedges—a
necessary precaution for them who never wore breeches but
only a small kilt or petticoat which falls down to the knees;
and during this operation they returned the fire of the English
with admirable firmness and constancy. The hedge down
they leapt into the enclosures sword in hand with an inconceivable intrepidity, and broke down the English battalions
with even greater carnage than (not turning their backs as
they did at the battle of Gladsmuir or Prestonpans) they
allowed themselves to be cut in pieces without moving out of
their places. We saw platoons. of forty to fifty men fall in
an instant under the strokes of the swords of the Highlanders,
always holding themselves firm and keeping their ranks and
files to such a degree that they were cleared by the strokes of
the sabres. In short, the Highlanders pursued them across
three rows of enclosures forward to a moorland, which was
behind, all giving way before them, and carrying all before
them like lightning. They only made one single prisoner,
that was the courier of the Duke of Cumberland, who declared
that the Duke his master would have been killed if the pistol,
which a Highlander presented at his head, had not missed
fire. The Prince had the politeness on the spot to send him
back to his master. We have no means of knowing the loss
of the English in this affair, which some made to amount to
six hundred men. We lost only a dozen of Highlanders who,
after having crossed the enclosures, continued the pursuit with

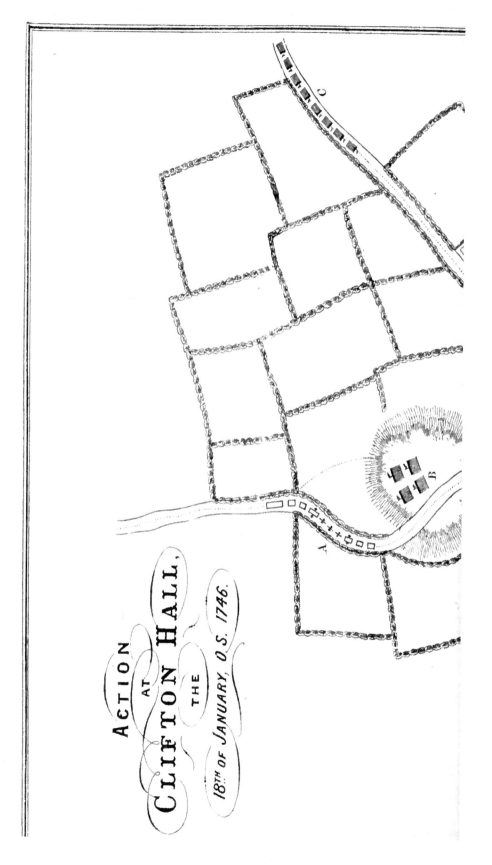

ACTION AT CLIFTON HALL, THE 18TH OF JANUARY, O.S. 1746.

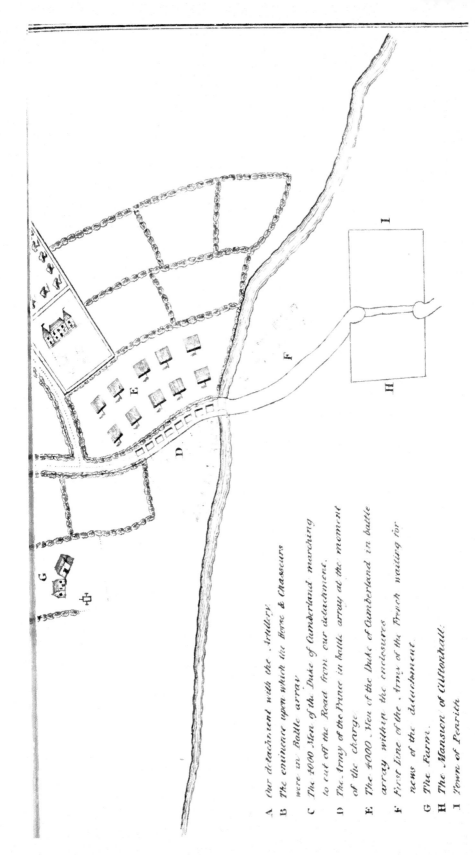

A Our detachment with the Artillery.
B The eminence upon which the Horse & Chasseurs
   were in Battle array
C The 4000 Men of the Duke of Cumberland marching
   to cut off the Road from our detachment.
D The Army of the Prince in battle array at the moment
   of the charge.
E The 4000 Men of the Duke of Cumberland in battle
   array within the enclosures.
F First line of the Army of the French waiting for
   news of the detachment.
G The Farm.
H The Mansion of Cliftonhall.
I Town of Penrith.

too much ardour to the moor. Our army did not leave Clifton Hall till some hours after nightfall, but the artillery was sent back at the commencement of the affair with orders to continue their route to Carlisle without stopping at Penrith. We learned from the courier that the Duke of Cumberland having given all the trumpeters and kettle drummers of his cavalry to these light horses, had hoped to retard the march of our detachment with the artillery; and for little if we had fallen into that snare we would have been lost without recourse, for in half an hour later the Duke of Cumberland would have found himself between Scotland and our army, and our communication with Scotland would have been cut off.

As we feared much the junction of the army of Marshal Wade with the four thousand men which the Duke of Cumberland had conducted to Clifton Hall by forced marches for the purpose of harassing us in our retreat, as well as the arrival of the rest of his army which he had left behind him, ours marched the whole night, and it arrived at Carlisle towards seven o'clock in the morning of the 19th of December. The next day, before it was light, we departed from Carlisle, where the Prince left the unfortunate M. Townly with his regiment of Englishmen, which he had had at Manchester, to command in the city, and M. Hamilton to command in the citadel, with some companies of the regiment of the Duke of Perth, promising them to return back to their aid in a few days, although it appeared morally impossible to do so; we ourselves using all our efforts to save ourselves from the entire force of England which was upon the point of uniting together. I was never able to comprehend the idea of risking the sacrifice of these unfortunate victims which we had left at Carlisle. The Prince was not under the control of any one; besides he could not hope that they would be able to hold such a miserable place against the united armies of the Duke of Cumberland and Marshal Wade provided with powerful artillery.

This place could not resist a cannonade for a quarter of

an hour, knowing, above all, with what facility we had captured it on our entering into England. It was in no degree susceptible of defence; and a thousand times taken the intrenchments were razed to the ground; moreover, no one could doubt but that the Duke of Cumberland would immediately undertake the siege; and Lord John Drummond not being on the march to join us, we proceeded to ensconce ourselves in the centre of Scotland to unite ourselves to him. Some pretended that it was a political stroke to leave that unfortunate garrison as a bait to allure the Duke of Cumberland, and prevent him following us closely, in order to afford us time to retire tranquilly without being molested by the English armies; by others that it was from a spirit of vengeance against the English nation—no person of distinction in England, of all those who had invited the Prince to make a descent upon Great Britain, having declared openly in his favour by attaching their fortunes to his as the Scots had done.

It appeared that our audacity and our rashness had absorbed and turned the heads of the generous English, those most distinguished for their talents, capacity, and experience; and they were entirely disconcerted.

The conduct of Marshal Wade appeared incomprehensible. He had only ten or twelve leagues to march to cut off our retreat to Scotland, which is the distance there is from Newcastle-upon-Tyne to Carlisle; and when our retreat was decided upon at Derby, we were distant from Carlisle well nigh to a hundred leagues. In the meantime, in spite of the orders which he had received from the Duke of Cumberland to that effect, and the vast disproportion of the route he had to make, compared to that we had to depart from England, he arrived at Kendal too late to throw himself between us and Scotland, by some hours. Every one in our army was convinced, by the position of General Wade, that there was no means of leaving England without coming to a battle with him in our retreat. This would not at all have displeased the Highlanders, in the good disposition they were in to fight; but even a victory then would not have been of great use to us, and it could have availed us nothing, because in England it was not possible to augment the number of our army, and this was the principal object in order to render it more redoubtable.

Having left Carlisle, the 20th December, at three o'clock in the morning, we arrived on the banks of the river Esk, which separates Scotland from England, towards two o'clock in the afternoon. The ford of that river, which ordinarily is not deep, was swollen by the quantity of rain that had fallen during several weeks, even to four feet of water. In the meantime it was indispensable to pass without delay at the ford, for fear lest the continuation of the rain during the night might render it altogether impracticable. Our position was become highly critical, having not only to face all the English troops, but moreover the Hessians, Swedes, and six thousand Dutch, of the garrisons of Dendermende and Tournay, who were landed in England.

The passage of this river was all that one could wish to see—most beautiful. Our cavalry formed themselves in the river about twenty-five paces above the entrance of the ford, where our infantry would have to pass, to break the force of the current, and the Highlanders formed files of ten or twelve men abreast, entwining one another's arms to sustain them reciprocally against the great rapidity of the river, leaving the intervals between the ranks, to let the water escape. There was, besides, some of the cavalry spread in the river below the ford, for the purpose of keeping up and saving those that might be carried away by the violence of the stream. This was like a paved street which traversed the river, the Highlanders, for the most part, not having more than their heads above the water. According to this arrangement, our army crossed the Esk in about an hour's time, without losing a single man; and there were none but some girls who were carried down by the rapidity of the river, who had resolved to follow the fate of their sweethearts. They made fires to dry themselves on getting out of the water; and the pipers having sounded their bagpipes, they all began to dance, testifying much joy on revisiting their native land, and forgetting the troubles with which they had been beset, and what they had experienced since their departure from Derby.

We entered England the 8th of November, and we left it the 20th of December, the Prince's birth-day, without losing but forty men, including therein the dozen in the affair at Clifton Hall, either by disease or mauraders, who never failed to be overpowered by the English peasantry, all outrageous enemies of the Prince, but with hearts too cowardly to dare to take up arms against us;—although the different Provinces through which we had passed in England would have been able easily to form an army of a hundred thousand militia to oppose us; they wanted neither the hatred nor the good will to destroy us, but the courage and resolution to expose themselves to the strokes of the Highlanders' swords. The fright of the English was inconceivable, and to a degree that seemed as if their heads were turned altogether. M. Cameron, of Lochiel, on entering the lodging which had been marked out for him, his hostess, a woman of years, fell at his feet supplicating him with hands joined, and with a flood of tears, to take away her life, but to spare those of her two little children. He demanded of her if she was mad, and to explain herself. She replied that every one said that the Highlanders ate children, and made them their ordinary food. M. Cameron having assured her that they would do no evil to her or her little ones, or any other body whoever they might be,—she fixed her eyes for a moment upon him with an air of surprise, and at once opened quickly a closet, calling out with a loud voice—"Come out, my children, the Gentleman will not eat you." The children came out immediately from the closet in which she had concealed them, and fell at his knees.

They published in their newspapers in London, that we
had an army of dogs to fight, and that we were indebted for
our victory at Gladsmuir, or Prestonpans, to these dogs, which
flew with rage upon the English army. They described the
Highlanders as monsters with claws in place of hands. In
short, they did not cease daily to make stories about the
Highlanders, the most ridiculous and extravagant. In fact,
the English soldiers had good reason to believe us extraordinary men by the manner in which we had beaten them,
being so inferior to them in number, and probably to cover
their disgrace. They recounted to the country people romantic stories at the expense of the Highlanders; the farmers
repeating them to their wives improved upon the lies of the
soldiers, and growing by progression into the marvellous, they
became in the end brutes, so enormous, that there were none
but English peasants, a credulous people, and void of reflection, who could have allowed themselves to believe such
extravagancies. But there is nothing so absurd that you
may not easily make them believe. The placard which they
put up at London during the time that I was there, to see in
the theatre at Haymarket a man dancing in a pint bottle is one
proof of it. Every one ran there, at a crown a seat, even to
the Duke of Cumberland, who lost his sword in the hubbub.
But the actor more sensible than they, after having appeared
to beseech the assembly to grant him but a quarter of an hour
more before commencing his opening address, as soon as he
had realized some bags full of guineas for tickets, took himself off cleverly; leaving them to dance attendance waiting
till he should redeem his promise, and treating them as a
company of fools as they deserved. After this trait of credu-
lity, one ought no longer to be astonished at their ridiculousness and extravagance.

When everybody had passed the river Esk, the Prince
formed our army into two columns, of which one took the
road to Ecclefechan, conducted by the Prince; the other,

under the orders of Lord George Murray, took the route to go to the town of Annan. Lord Elcho, with the cavalry, took the middle road to Dumfries, a considerable town of Scotland, but full of calvinistic fanatics, who had seized some of our ammunition carriages left behind when we entered into England; we punished this town by making its inhabitants pay a very considerable fine. As there was not a town nearer to the ford than eight or ten miles, we were obliged to march all the night, and it had never ceased an instant to rain since the affair at Clifton Hall. The Highlanders should have sunk under these two nights' march in the middle of winter, in a time of frightful rain, and drenched as they were on leaving the river; but they were inured to fatigue, and of temperament strong and vigorous, making often five, six, or seven leagues a day our ordinary journeys in England, without ever leaving stragglers behind; and they would have been able even to destroy an army of ten thousand men of regular troops, in marching alone, if they had inclined always to follow us. We always had a principal object in the disposition of our marches—to keep the English constantly in uncertainty with regard to our movements, the towns to which we intended to go, and the roads we were to take; continually changing our course, it behoved them to remain in inaction until they should ascertain our true point of rendezvous for the rejunction of our columns, which made them lose a great deal of time.

The column conducted by Lord George (Murray) arrived the next day, in the morning, at Annan, where it rested the 22d, and reached Moffat the 23d. On the 24th it quitted the road which it had followed till then, which led directly to Edinburgh, and took a road across to the left to proceed to Glasgow, where its junction with that of the Prince was effected on the 26th, the column of the Prince having stopped the 21st at Ecclefechan, the 22d at Dumfries, and the 23rd took the route straight to Glasgow; and Lord Elcho with the cavalry reached that city the 25th, the morning watch after the arrival of these two columns. The Duke of Cumberland in uncertainty, by our movements, of our designs, gave over following us, and the two English armies halted at Carlisle.

Two officers in the service of France, Messieurs Brown and Gordon, who had been left at Carlisle, came to join us again on our arrival in Glasgow. They declared to the Prince that that city, with the citadel, had been taken on the morrow of our departure, and that they had not been able to resist twenty-four hours the heavy artillery of the enemy; and that the Duke of Cumberland granted in the capitulation of that garrison to spare their lives, and that they should not be brought to trial for having taken up arms. They added in their declaration that they had saved themselves from Carlisle the moment the capitulation had come to be signed. The army of the Duke of Cumberland was composed of the regiments of Ligonier, Richmond, Sinclair, Albemarle, Howard, Skelton, Bland, Sempill, Bligh, Douglas, Leslie, Bernard, Roper, Lowle, Johnson, Gower, Montague, Halifax, Granby, Cholmelondley, and Montague and Kingston Cavalry, these three last being newly raised, and a corps of a thousand men of unattached cavalry of the army of Marshal Wade, under the command of General Ogelthrope. Besides this there were six thousand Dutch, every regiment having eight hundred and twenty-four men, and the regiments of cavalry two hundred and seventy-three. The Chevalier Francis Geohagen, Colonel attached to the regiment of Lolly, an officer of spirit and merit, who was left sick at Carlisle, sent a trumpeter with a letter to the Commander-in-chief of the Dutch troops. ordering them, in name of the King of France, to retire in consequence of the capitulation of Tournay and Dendermonde, and they did so immediately; but the diminution in the number of the besieging army was of no benefit to the besieged. The garrison of Carlisle was thrown into the prisons in London; and the Duke of Cumberland, on his arrival there the

5th of January, had the extreme bad faith to hold, without regard to the capitulation which he had signed to maintain it, that he was not obliged in honour to keep a capitulation with rebels. Thus a dozen of these unfortunate officers of the English regiment, with Messieurs Townly and Hamilton at their head, were immediately hanged and quartered at London. The head of the unfortunate Townly still remains exposed on one of the gates of London named Temple Bar.*

The Prince at first seemed unwilling to believe the information of the Scotsmen, Messieurs Gordon and Brown. Some accused them of lies, but it was not those who had the least knowledge of fortifications. The Prince without doubt if he had foreseen the fate of those unfortunate victims, would have prevented it by evacuating this place in our retreat, the only course to take, not only for the sake of humanity, but for those who had made a sacrifice of their lives and their estates in attaching themselves to his fortune, but for his own particular interest, not having too many in his army. It is a cruelty over which it is necessary to cast a veil, not being able either to divine a motive for leaving those four hundred men at Carlisle, or to furnish an excuse for it.

*Some singular anecdotes are told in relation to these barbarous exhibitions. Horace Walpole, after the 16th August, 1746, in contempt, wrote—"We passed the new heads of Temple Bar, where people make traffic of letting spy-glasses at halfpenny a look." It was said with regard to the ghastly exhibitions which were allowed to remain so long at Temple Bar, that although the last heads, those of Colonel Townly and his faithful servant Fletcher, were placed there in 1746, there was still one remaining in March, 1772, twenty-six years afterwards.

Dr. Johnson relates "that he remembered once being with Goldsmith in Westminster Abbey, and that while surveying the Poets' Corner he said to him, 'Forsitan et nostrum nomen miscebitur istis.' When, he adds, we got to Temple Bar, he stopped me, pointed to the heads upon it, and slily whispered, 'Forsitan et nostrum nomen miscebitur *istis*,'" in allusion to Johnson's political principles, and perhaps his own. What a contrast to the measure of justice meted out to these poor misguided Scotchmen, compared to that extended to the Irish rebels of the present day, who have been equally, if not more, guilty of high treason, sedition, and felony, not to say agrarian outrage and murder.—ED.

Glasgow is the second city of Scotland for the number of its inhabitants and for the extent of its commerce. Our army sojourned there to recover from their fatigues, to the 2nd of January, when it departed in two columns, of which one took the route to Cumbernauld, where it passed the night; and the other went to Kilsyth. The Prince, by this movement, made it appear as if he intended to go to Edinburgh, with much more appearance than Lord Elcho, who, with the cavalry advanced himself forward as far as the town of Falkirk, which is not distant from it but five leagues. But the column which had passed the night at Kilsyth, quitted the next day in the morning the road to Edinburgh, and turning to the left, the two columns met each other in the evening at the village of Bannockburn, about half-a league from Stirling. It was the design of the Prince in throwing himself upon the side of Stirling, to accelerate his junction with Lord John Drummond, having ordered him to place himself at Alloa with the three thousand men, which he had under his command and to transport thither, at the sametime, the artillery and the ammunition which he had brought with him from France. The city of Stirling—protected by the castle where there was a strong garrison, under the command of General Blockeney, who was Governor of it—having refused to surrender, the Prince sent a part of his army, the 4th of January, to occupy the villages of St. Dennis and St. Ninians, to the south of Stirling, which were within cannon shot of the site of that town, and by that position it was blockaded and invested on all sides,—the bridge of stone on the river, north of the town, having been broken down by the English when General Cope was there with his army.

Lord George Murray, who always took charge of every thing and saw all, immediately on our arrival at Bannockburn, proceeded to Alloa, where Lord John Drummond had already arrived, in order to cause the forces and artillery—brought with him from France—to be despatched without loss of time to Stirling. After having inspected and given the necessary orders for transporting the guns, he returned the next day to Bannockburn, where he took eleven hundred men and established himself in a fixed post at Falkirk, a town about sixteen miles from Edinburgh, and about four from Bannockburn; having caused Lord Elcho to advance with the cavalry to occupy the city of Linlithgow, which is about twelve miles from Edinburgh, and about six from Falkirk. The rest of the army was cantoned in the villages of St. Dennis and St. Ninians, as well as at Bannockburn. which is about two miles from Stirling, where the Prince established his head quarters. Lord John Drummond came at length to Bannockburn with his regiment of Scotch Royals, and with five picquets of the Irish brigade; also Lord Lewis Gordon with six hundred men, vassals of his brother, the Duke of Gordon; M. Fraser, eldest son of Lord Lovat, with six hundred men, vassals of his father; M. the Earl of Cromarty, and his eldest son, Lord Macleod, with his vassals; the Mackenzies; and besides these, many other Highlanders of the Macintoshes and Farquharsons, in so much, that by this reinforcement, our army amounted to eight thousand men, and found itself all of a sudden double the number which we had in England.

What a misfortune that the Prince had not had these eight thousand men at Derby; they would have been able to succeed in causing him to be crowned at London. Moderating his impatience, to have remained in Scotland until his adherents had had time to come from the more distant provinces to Edinburgh to join him, he would have been able to have had such numbers, and then, his affairs being properly established in Scotland, he could have gone in quest of adventures in England. It would appear that Lord John was detained in Scotland by the difficulty of transporting the six pieces of cannon sent with him from France, and the fear of leaving them to fall into the hands of the English. The chimerical and imaginary idea which he attached to the artillery, and their utility on all occasions, and the absolute necessity of having it is greatly above the reality—and I have no doubt that in time an army will believe itself lost when they have not these enormous masses to drag after them with infinite embarrassment, in the same manner as it causes infantry to tremble when they have not cavalry to protect their wings — which the Highlanders always treat with sovereign contempt, on account of the facility with which they have always put it to flight, throwing it into disorder in an instant by strokes of their sabres, upon the horses' heads, as I have already said.

The greater part of the world adopt general rules blindly, without examining and searching out their application to particular cases. It is certainly necessary that an army of regular troops should now have attached to it a strong force of artillery. They have given up Clan arms for muskets; and it appears by the victories gained in this last war, solely by a great superiority of artillery, that they wished to leave muskets for cannons, establishing the maxim for armies, that regarding only the places which are strongest in artillery, they should extinguish the fire of the weakest. I do not know whether this new fancy or taste is well or ill founded; but I am very certain that ours has been very burdensome to us, and even injurious. A regular army has need of artillery in order to reduce fortified places, which were met with at every pace upon ordinary theatres of war for many ages in Europe; but in Great Britain there is not a fortified town; only two in Scotland, the two castles of Stirling and Edinburgh, which are situated upon the summits of high rocks, peaks of so great altitude that there is not to be found in the neighbourhood any ground parallel, to establish a battery of cannon which could play with effect. It is only with mortars or by famine that it could ever be possible to reduce these two castles. It is surprising that the court of

France was so ill informed about the "*locale*" of Scotland as to send us cannons in place of mortars, of which we had need to enable us to carry on sieges. The field pieces which we had taken at Gladsmuir or Prestonpans sufficed to force the small forts and houses. The artillery, in place of serving us, incommoded considerably our army, retarding continually our marches. Every firearm was directly contrary to the natural dispositions of the Highlanders, who are quick, ardent, and impetuous in their attacks. A light weapon was that which suited them best: to leave them to languish, that was to weaken their fury. It is necessary at all times to consult the dispositions of those we have to command, and to conform ourselves to particular customs. If we were resting at a certain distance to fire, in place of joining on the instant the enemy, the sword in hand of two thousand men of regular troops, who are disciplined only to fire, and accustomed, too, to light weapons, would easily beat four thousand Highlanders. Their manner of fighting is congenial to brave but undisciplined people. They advance with rapid strides to the enemy; keeping up their fire till the muzzles of their guns meet, they immediately throw away their muskets to the ground; then they draw their swords, and holding their poinards in their left hand with their bucklers, they rush rapidly on the enemy through the smoke of their discharge. When they are at the point of the enemy's bayonets, bending down on their left knee they cover by their posture their bodies with their bucklers, which receive the blows of the bayonets, which they ward off and parry at the same time with the strokes of their sabres. Being once in the midst of the bayonets, and mixed with the ranks of the enemy, the soldier having no longer any defensive weapon, the issue of the battle is decided in an instant, and the carnage ensues, the Highlanders causing two men to fall at once, one with their dirk in their left hand, and the other with the stroke of their sabre.

The practice of the Highlanders of throwing their muskets to the ground is perhaps justified by their reasonings. On gaining a victory they recover their guns which incommoded them in their manœuvre, as well as their cross belts, and they picked them up again at the same time with the arms of the vanquished. If they lose the battle they have no farther use for guns. They exemplified that bravery sometimes can supply the place of discipline, as discipline that of bravery. Their attack is terrible—the best troops in Europe could sustain with difficulty their first onset; and if they are assailed with the swords of the Highlanders their rout is inevitable.

On the 6th of January we opened the trenches before the city of Stirling, under the direction of M. Grant, but the threatening alone to lay siege to it induced the magistrates of that city to repair to Bannockburn to capitulate, and the Prince having granted them the conditions they asked, we took possession of Stirling the next day. The castle was not comprehended therein. General Blockeney replied very politely to the summons of the Prince, "That certainly His Royal Highness would have a very bad opinion of him if he could believe him capable of surrendering the castle with so much cowardice."

An army of about thirteen thousand men, composed of that which had been the best troops of the armies of Wade and the Duke of Cumberland, came into Scotland, under the orders of M. Hawley, Lieutenant-General, the first division of which arrived at Edinburgh on the 4th of January, with General Husk; and General Hawley arrived there the 6th. The whole army of General Hawley being collected together in that city, General Husk started for Linlithgow on the 13th, with the fine old regiments of Munro, Cholmondeley, Price, Ligonier, and Battereau, and with those of the Hamilton and Gardiner dragoons, the wreck of those which had escaped at the battle of Gladsmuir or Prestonpans. This first division of the English army entered into this small town by one side, while Lord Elcho with our cavalry departed by the other, to join himself under Lord George (Murray) at Falkirk. On the 14th the regiments of Howard, Pulteney, and Barrel went to Borrowstonness, which is half-way between Edinburgh and Linlithgow; and they were followed on the 15th by the regiments of Fleming, Blackeney, and a battalion of Sinclairs. On the 16th General Hawley came with all his army to encamp at Falkirk, having in his train two field pieces; and Lord George Murray, at his approach, returned again to Bannockburn, with the corps which he had commanded for some time at Falkirk.

M. Mirabelle de Gordon, a French engineer, a Knight of the Order of St. Louis, was sent into Scotland with Lord John Drummond, and he arrived on the 6th at Stirling. There were formed of him, at first, great hopes of his being able to reduce the castle, which would annoy the Highlanders much in preventing their going and returning to their own country, believing that an engineer of France of a certain age, and decorated with an order, behoved necessarily to have experience, talents, and capacity, but they discovered, unfortunately too late, that these requisites of his genius were very limited, and that he had not the shadow of judgment, discernment, or good sense; his figure being as ridiculous as his spirits—the Highlanders changed his name of Mirabelle, and called him always M. Admirable.

M. Grant had already given the Prince his project of attacking the castle—proposing to open the trenches, and establish his batteries in the cemetery, on the side of the city which looked towards the gate of the castle. He assured the Prince that this was the only point where they could find a parallel nearly on a level with the batteries of the enemy, and that in battering in breach, the half moon which defended the entry to the castle by a battery in the cemetery, the rubbish of this work would fill the ditch, and render an assault practicable on that side, when the breach would be made and the defences destroyed on the side of the gate. He added that it was quite useless to think of making an attack otherwise, from the impossibility of succeeding in it, the hills in the neighbourhood of the castle being from forty to fifty feet less elevated than the castle, and our cannon could not operate with effect, and their batteries would play into ours. Moreover, that supposing even it was possible to make a breach in the side there, none could ever mount there to the assault, the rock upon which the castle is built being, all around, very high, very steep, and almost perpendicular, except on the side of the town, opposite the cemetery.

The inhabitants of Stirling having made remonstrances to the Prince, that in establishing our batteries in the cemetery, the fire of the batteries from the Castle would reduce their city to ashes, the Prince consulted M. Mirabelle to know if there was not another way to take the castle, by an attack otherwise than in the cemetery. As it is always a distinguishing mark of ignorant people never to find anything difficult, not even things impossible, M. Mirabelle undertook the matter at once with assurances of success. He opened immediately trenches upon the hill to the north of the castle, where he had not above five inches of depth of ground, without finding all at once hard rock ; and it was necessary to supply the defect of the ground by bales of wool and by sacks full of earth, which we were obliged to fetch from a distance, so that the trenches were so bad that we lost many men, sometimes as many as twenty-five a day. The six pieces of cast-iron guns sent from France arrived on the 24th at Stirling, of which two were eighteen, two twelve, and two six pounders.

The Prince gave orders in the evening of the 16th, that all the army should next day at early dawn, be under arms upon a plain a little to the east of Bannockburn, in order to be reviewed, and no one suspected that he had any other design in this general review than to choose a field of battle, and make a reconnoissance of the locality—a thing much more essential, as the English army then encamped at Falkirk, about two leagues from us, could in a moment have advanced from the other side to attack us. When he had finished his review, about six o'clock in the morning, he made his army wheel to the right to form in column, and caused it immediately defile, taking the circuitous roads on our right, without any person in the army being able to penetrate his design, so much the more as he did not seem 'at first to be taking the roads approaching to the English army. The Highlanders had a manœuvre very simple and convenient for a small army composed of undisciplined men. They formed themselves in battle array in three ranks, and by one at the right and one at the left, they formed into column, marching by ranks of three men; thence they found themselves at once in battle array, by one at the right or one at the left, and left their ancient and simple manœuvre rather than learn imperfectly to make four squares to form themselves in order of battle, and break through divisions, &c., which they would not be able to execute without disorder or confusion. It is not in the heat of action that one ought to pretend to discipline a corps, and change their ancient habits. It is necessary for that to take a long training, and in time of peace.

Our army transported itself to Dunnipace, across the country, and by cross roads, leaving the great road from Stirling to Falkirk, far distant on our left; and making a grand detour to conceal from the English the knowledge of our march.

Having crossed the village of Dunnipace, about two o'clock in the afternoon, which is at a distance of about a quarter of a league from Falkirk, we found ourselves all of a sudden upon the heights of that city, in sight of the English army, not being farther distant than about three hundred toises from their camp, before General Hawley knew of our departure from Bannockburn. One may judge of their surprise on seeing us appear. They ran immediately to arms, and they ascended with precipitation, to the side of an eminence between us and the city of Falkirk. A strong wind prevailed, with a great rain full in the face, which the Highlanders, by their position, had in the back, in place as it blew full in the faces of the English, and the rain pelting in their eyes blinded them; they had besides this the inconvenience of the smoke of our firing, and the rain pouring into their priming pans, the half of their muskets would not give fire. The English endeavoured ineffectually to gain the advantage of the wind by deploying on their left; but the Prince, by his strategy, had on his part the same care, and the same attention to preserve that advantage.

General Hawley arranged his army in order of battle, in two lines, being three regiments *(c.)* of infantry, in a depth of a foot of the ascent, *(e.)* and his cavalry *(g.)* was placed before his infantry, to that of the left of his first line. The English commenced the attack by a corps of cavalry of a hundred men, who advanced quite safely against the right of our army, and did not stop till about the distance of twenty paces from our first line, on purpose to await our fire. The Highlanders, as they had engaged, as much as they could, not to fire till about touching muzzles, at the moment the cavalry halted, let go their discharge, which brought down to the ground about twenty-four men, having, every one aimed at a horseman. The commandant of the corps of cavalry was of the number, having advanced some paces before his troop. This cavalry closing up immediately their ranks and files, opened by our discharge, formed a buttress to their horses, and rushed upon the Highlanders at a grand trot, piercing into their ranks, driving all before them and trampling the Highlanders under their horses' feet. Then ensued a combat the most remarkable and surprising. The Highlanders extended on the earth, pitched their poinards into the horses' bellies; others seizing the cavalry men by their dresses, and pulling them down, slew them with strokes of their poinards; many used their pistols, but there were few that had elbow room to be able to wield their swords. M. Macdonald, of Clan Ranald, chief of one of the Clans of that name, told me that being extended on the ground, below a dead horse, which had fallen upon him, without his being able to disengage himself, he saw a dismounted horseman in shackles with a Highlander, who held one another round the middle, when, for his good luck, the Highlander being by far the stronger, threw the horseman to the ground, and having killed him with his dirk, he then came to his assistance and tore him with difficulty, from below the horse. In short, the resistance of the Highlanders was so incredibly obstinate, that the English cavalry, after having been for some time in their ranks, pell mell with them, were in the end repulsed, and forced to retreat. But the Highlanders not slacking the fight, pursued them vigorously with sabre strokes, running after them as quick as their horses, and leaving them not a moment's respite to be able to recover from their fright; in so much, that the English cavalry rushed through their own infantry in the battlefield behind them; there it immediately fell into disorder, and dragged their army with them in their rout.* The night began to fall when the English army entered the town, and immediately we saw fires lighted through the whole camp. From what every one could judge, the enemy had retired, and that we had not gained a complete and solid victory; the honour of guarding the field of battle had ad-

---

* This is not the first time that cavalry, in battle, in front of infantry, has caused a rout. Machiavel relates that in the war between the Florentines and the Pisans, at the battle of Santo Regolo, the Florentines occasioned their own defeat by their own cavalry,—which having been drawn up in battle order in front of their army, and charged briskly by the enemy, was thrown into disorder, and forced to fall back upon their own infantry, which put the Florentine army immediately to rout. He cites at the sametime the affair of Tiberius Gracchus, &c. The battle of Falkirk confirms me in my opinion that it is a very bad disposition to place cavalry in front.

vanced us nothing. We had no reason to believe that we had lost the battle since the English army had retired; but the opinion in their camp was that they regarded the battle as indecisive, and ready to be renewed next day in the morning.

It was our good luck that the enemy did not perceive the disorder which was spread through all our army, which Colonel John Roy Stewart was the innocent cause of, by his too great precaution and foresight. The Highlanders were in the greatest confusion—dispersed suddenly, and all the different corps intermingled. Besides, the darkness of the night added to our confusion; it had already become so great that they had left the field of battle, whether it was that they believed it lost, or whether it was to find a shelter from the tempestuous weather which prevailed. It is very often more dangerous to check the flight and impetuosity of soldiers, the best of whom are but machines, and still more of undisciplined masses who do not pay attention to orders, than to leave them to run all hazards to extricate themselves. The Highlanders, those who had not already descended into the plain, halted on the eminence. This was what gave birth to the disorder, which ensued with the quickness of lightning.

I met, by chance, Colonel Brown of the Irish brigade, and proposed to him that we should stick together to participate in the same lot; he agreed to it, but he told me at the same time that the Prince having charged him to carry some order, he wished to find him to deliver the answer. After having searched a long time in vain without finding any one who could give us the least intelligence of him, having found his body guards near the battle field, in a cottage alongside the eminence, with their commandant, Lord Elcho, who knew no more than the others anything of the Prince, the night having closed in and being very dark, with an adverse rain, we took the resolution at last to retire to the castle of M. Primrose of Dunnipace, about a quarter of a league from

Falkirk, having for a guide, a troop of Highlanders, who were going to take the same road

Arrived at the castle, we there found Lord Lewis Gordon, brother of the Duke of Gordon, M. Fraser, son of Lord Lovat, and six or seven other Chiefs of Clans, but none of them knew what had become of their regiments. Other officers came from time to time, all ignorant of the fate of the battle, and equally in doubt whether we had lost or gained. Towards eight o'clock at night M. MacDonald of Glengary came there to join us, and relieved the despondency of every one by announcing to us, for now certain, that it was the most complete victory we had ever gained, and that the English, in place of being in their camp, had fled in disorder towards Edinburgh ; he added, in confirmation of this news, that he had left the Prince in the town of Falkirk, occupying the same lodging which had been that of General Hawley, and that the Prince had sent him express to Dunnipace to advertise all his force to repair to Falkirk next morning by break of day. It would be impossible, in our situation, to know the extreme joy that this agreeable surprise made us feel. The enemy in his retreat having abandoned to us all their tents and baggage, in spite of the darkness and bad weather, their camp was immediately pillaged by the Highlanders, and the booty carried off. The enemy had six hundred men killed, and we took seven hundred prisoners. It was Lord Kilmarnock who discovered the retreat of the English. At the point of the place, having a party of his pioneers in the suburbs of Falkirk, the Prince had sent him to make a reconnoissance of the enemy, and his lordship, having approached to the road to Edinburgh, in passing the town of Falkirk by his sentries across the fields, he saw the English army, which, seized with a terrible panic, had fled with all their legs in the greatest possible disorder. Lord Kilmarnock returned immediately to the Prince to give him an account of this fortunate discovery, having always remained upon the field of battle, in spite of the frightful tempest of wind and rain. But he then descended from the eminence, at half-past seven o'clock at night, entered immediately the town of Falkirk, and sent forward a force, which they were able to collect promptly, to harrass the English in their flight, from which their army was not as yet far distant.

The enemy not having been able to avail himself of his artillery during the action, nor to carry it off with him in his retreat, we found next day six pieces half way up the hill *(e.)* which he had not had time to carry up to the top of the aclivity. He lost many men in the pond at the foot of the eminence, the corn fields being there strewed with dead bodies more than anywhere else. The English in their flight made a prisoner in a very singular way. M. Macdonald, major of one of the regiments of that name, having dismounted an English officer, took possession of his horse, which was very beautiful, and immediately mounted it. When the English cavalry took to flight, the horse ran off with the unfortunate Macdonald, in spite of all his efforts to restrain him, and he never stopped till he was at the head of a regiment of which, to all appearance, his master was the commandant. One can imagine the miserable and laughable figure the poor Macdonald made, seeing himself thus the victim of his ambition for a fine horse, which cost him his life, which he lost upon the scaffold.

If General Hawley had had the coolness and presence of mind, when he saw our army upon the height, to have reflected calmly and to have examined the disadvantages and inconveniences which he would have had to give us battle all at once, and he had remained in his own camp prepared to defend himself, if we had chosen to attack him, the Prince would have been terribly disconcerted, and I don't know which course we should have been able to take; his army would not have been able to pass the night in open air in a frightful tempest; and it would have been a kind of victory for

General Hawley, if the Prince had been obliged to retrace his steps, by a night march in the midst of the most horrible weather that can be imagined. But it is in the nature of man, that the occurrence of anything unexpected and unforeseen, makes more or less impression upon his mind, according to the importance of the matter, and the consequences which it is calculated to produce. There are not many enterprises well combined with accuracy, and conducted in the same manner in the execution, that do not succeed. Some men have the perception of ideas more clear than others, and are affected and struck with the same object more or less, according to the tone of their temperament or the vivacity of their imaginations. Some apprehend in an instant, a complicated and doubtful affair, and seize upon the true plan, while others take a long time to reflect, before coming to a solution of the difficulty, although they have, at the same time, a judgment and penetration equally just and solid, different the one from the other, solely by the perception that they require to comprehend it. It requires of every one, more or less time, to arrest the torrent of different ideas, which present themselves in a crowd, to the imagination in a pressing case, and to lay hold and fix upon the best. In a surprise, it is necessary to adopt a plan on the instant, the enemy not giving time for reflection; and it is a great and essential quality, in a general of an army, to have correct and ready discernment and judgment in his decisions. Coolness, perhaps, often supplies a defect in the quickness of imagination, and finds out resources in troublesome embarrassments; but hot blood, which is good at the head of grenadiers, in a surprise, ferments the mechanism of spirit with the faculty of thinking, and sees all trouble. Surprises always succeed. We don't find two Marshals Luxembourg twice in the same age.* Deceived at Steinkirk by his spy, the Secretary of the

---

* Those alone, says Suntse, the Chinese General, possess truly the art of rightly governing troops who have knowledge, and who know to render their knowledge formidable; who have acquired an unbounded authority;

Prince of Orange, who commanded him not to be alarmed at the next day seeing appear a great body of troops, and that it was only a general foraging that he wished to make, which, however, was all the army of the allies commanded by the Prince of Orange, who had discovered the treachery of his Secretary, and had forced him to write that letter with a pistol at his throat. In spite of the surprise, M. the Marshal of Luxembourg, after having been a long time before being able to persuade himself of the falsehood of the information of his spy, knew in the same moment to take measures so judicious that he had the Prince of Orange as if he had taken him in a net. We see few examples parallel to this in history. A truly great warrior masters events, in place of being mastered by them; and when he is surprised, he surprises the enemy himself.

The bad weather which was so favourable to us during the battle, in enabling us to gain the victory, was very prejudicial in the retreat, impeding us in the pursuit of the enemy in his rout, and dispersing that army entirely, without leaving a vestige of it in Scotland,—this would have given us repose and tranquility for a long time in Scotland, this army being composed of old regiments, and of the best troops the English had.

The next day, the 18th, the tempest continued throughout

who do not allow themselves to be abashed by an event however embarrassing it may possibly be; who execute nothing with precipitation; who carry it out even when they are surprised, with the coolness which they ordinarily have in premeditated actions, and in cases foreseen a long time before; and who act always in every case that occurs, with that promptitude which is not to be acquired but as the fruit of ability, joined to a lengthened experience. Such is the strength of these warriors. In the thick of a melee and a rout they appear. They know how to preserve order, which nothing is able to interrupt. They produce strength even in the bosom of weakness. They elicit courage and valour in the midst of cowardice and pusillanimity. But to know how to preserve a marvellous order, in the midst of disorder, that cannot be done without having made, beforehand, the deepest reflections of all events, that could possibly happen.

the whole journey, with the same violence, and with torrents of adverse rain, so frightful, that no one could budge out of his lodging. Having been sent to the residence of the Prince towards seven o'clock in the evening, and finding nobody there in his ante-chamber, at the moment when I intended to return to my own lodging, M. Sullivan came out of the cabinet of the Prince, and told me that the bad weather having been the cause of their having left still upon the field of battle the cannon taken from the enemy, without having there any force to guard them, he begged me to conduct thither, under my charge, a guard of a sergeant and twenty men to pass the night there—that I would find them below all ready to march. I departed with this detachment, the sergeant carrying a lantern, but the candle was soon blown out, and by this accident we directly lost our road— wandering for a long time, at the foot of the height, among heaps of dead bodies, which their pallor rendered visible, in spite of the darkness and obscurity of a night the most dark. Besides, the disagreeableness added to this picture of horrors, the wind and the rain beat full in our faces. I even remarked a trembling and quivering sensation in my horse, which seemed to start with fear, when he was forced to put down his feet upon the heads of carcasses and trample them down. My task being finished, after having been a long time among these heaps of carcasses, before finding out the place where the cannon were, on my return to Falkirk, I felt myself relieved of a load, but the horrible spectacle was present with me for a long time, and vividly impressed my mind. How inconsistent is man! We see during a battle our best friends fall dead by our side, as many times it had happened to myself, without our being sensibly affected with grief and regret, at the moment, for their unhappy fate, and we are seized with horror, when we go with indifference, through a field of battle, in which the sight of dead bodies is repugnant to nature, although while living they had been unknown to us.

BATTLE OF FALKIRK

17TH JANUARY, OS 1746

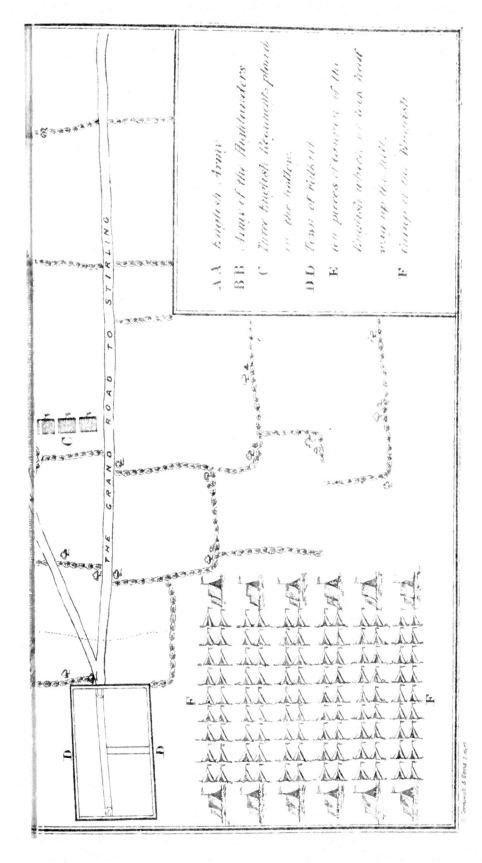

THE GRAND ROAD TO STIRLING

A A English Army
B B Arms of the Highlanders
C Three English Regiments placed
on the hollow
D D Town of ridiret
E ten pieces of cannon of the
English which in their retreat
were up the hills
F Camp of the English

Cornwell & Beard Lith.

How much does man differ from himself, acccording to the positions in which he finds himself placed. The Prince received news from Edinburgh, at every moment, with details of the consternation and panic-struck terror of the English in their flight. We learned that for several days after their defeat they had not recovered again from their fright, and that, upon a review of their resources of war, they had not four thousand men assembled at Edinburgh of the thirty or forty thousand of which their army was composed. The friends of the Prince exhorted him to repair thither with all diligence to disperse the remnant of the English army, and again to take possession of that city. This is what appeared to every one the only sensible course which the Prince had to follow; but we see that it was much more easy to gain a victory than to know how to profit by it. The gaining of a battle is very often the effect of mere chance; but to derive from a victory all the advantages of which it is susceptible, it is necessary to have great genius, much capacity, and superior talents; and it is in this that the great warrior shows himself particularly. It is certain that the vanquished can always derive great advantages from the negligence of the victors.*

On the 19th, the weather having become fine, it was natural to suppose that we should take the route to Edinburgh; but what fatal blindness! in place of pursuing an enemy vanquished, and in disorder, the Prince decided on returning to Bannockburn for the purpose of continuing the siege of the Castle of Stirling. This was the result of a consultation with that mad-cap M. Mirabelle, who promised the reduction of the

---

* We ought to have pursued the English with the rapidity of a torrent, in order that they might not have had time to recover themselves; always at their heels, and without leaving them an opportunity of rallying themselves; without dreaming of realizing the fruits of our victory until their entire defeat had placed us in a situation to make it avail at leisure and quietly; but one may say as Maherbal said to Hannibal, "Vincere scis, Annibal, uti victoria nescis."—*Livy*, book xxii. chap. 51.—"You know how to conquer, Hannibal, but not how to use your victory."—ED.

castle in forty-eight hours. The possession of that fort was not in the least degree essential to us; on the contrary, it was much more to our advantage that this castle should remain in the hands of the enemy, in order to restrain the Highlanders, and prevent them from returning, at pleasure, to their own country, for fear of being made prisoners, in passing before this castle, as a part of the Highlanders had done many a time before, when they found themselves loaded with spoils of the English, in order that they might place their booty under concealment. This fatal resolution of returning to Stirling gave occasion to Mr. Peter Smith, the Purveyor of our army, saying "that we had never made but blunders upon blunders, but that fortunately the good God had always turned these blunders to our advantage." In the meantime this ugly and gross blunder in not pursuing briskly the enemy, and of our not being close continually at their heels to disperse them entirely, without leaving so much as that there should remain one single Englishman upon Scottish ground, would have never been advantageous to us, and could not have failed, moreover, sooner or later to prove our destruction. Effects, far from corresponding to their causes, often produce a result entirely contrary to that which the appearance promised. Who could have imagined that six pieces of clumsy Cannon which the Court of France sent us should have caused our destruction? It is nevertheless true, had it not been for these cannon we should have never dreamed of undertaking the siege of the Castle of Stirling. Nobody ever thought of making a siege without artillery. As a consequence, the united advice of all would have been, after the victory at Falkirk, to destroy totally the English army by pursuing the enemy, and regaining possession of Edinburgh, the only course which would have naturally entered the mind of every one; not the having possession of that castle, which could be attempted to be done only in spite of good sense and judgment; and without cannon there would not have been that temptation.

The trenches, opened upon a hill to the north of the castle by Mirabelle, advanced very slowly, not finding there but a surface of earth, and we lost there a great many men, particularly the Irish piquets which were there destroyed. What distress to see these brave men perish uselessly by the rashness and ignorance of Mirabelle! These piquets who had conducted themselves at the battle of Falkirk with distinguished bravery and intrepidity, preserving themselves always in order while our whole army was dispersed, and presenting themselves to the enemy with a bold front, keeping them in check, ought to have been reserved for a better occasion.

At length, on the 30th of January, Mirabelle, with a childish impatience to discharge his battery, caused it to be unmasked as soon as he had three embrasures finished, of six of which it ought to have been composed, and our battery immediately commenced firing very briskly with these three pieces of cannon, but with very little force, producing very little effect upon the batteries of the castle, which, having a greater elevation than ours—where the enemy saw even to the shoe-buckles of the gunners—their descending shot dismounted immediately our cannon, and in less than half an hour it became necessary to abandon entirely our battery, nobody being able to come near it; besides that our guns being pointed high could do no execution. Thus the work of three weeks, which had prevented us from improving the advantages at Falkirk, and which had cost us the lives of many brave men, was in an instant tumbled down like a pack of cards, levelled to the ground like an old hulk, and our cannon dismounted. We ought to render justice to the merit and good conduct of General Blackeney, who, seeing our ignorance by the position of our attack, did not molest us during our work. Being well assured that from that side we could not be formidable to him, he temporized like an able man, and left us to go on, in order to make us lose the highly precious moments which would have been much better employed in the pursuit of the enemy, knowing well that he was master of demolishing our battery whenever he chose, and reducing it in half an hour's time to a heap of earth.

This blunder, in amusing ourselves before this castle, in place of pursuing the enemy, of which the punishment followed close at hand, was the first epoch of our mischances; till then fortune having appeared blindly to favour us. The English soldiers in their rout were so dispersed throughout the country that, during five days after the battle, with difficulty were they able to re-assemble four thousand men at Edinburgh, which, by our bad conduct, served them as a rallying point, and from which proceeded all our disasters in the long run. The enemy not having been briskly pursued, by little and little recovered from their consternation, and regained courage, from our inactivity and supineness, and rejoined their standards at length in the capital; in so much, that by the reinforcement of two regiments of infantry, the Sempils and the Scots Fusiliers, and the regiment of dragoons of Bland and St. George, with the light cavalry of Kingston, detached from the army of Marshal Wade, in eight or ten days their army became stronger than it had been at the battle of Falkirk.

General Cope enjoyed with a sensible pleasure the defeat of General Hawley, his brother officer. He had, according to the English fashion, opened bettings in all the coffee-houses in London, even to the sum of ten thousand guineas, that the first General, whom they should send to command in Scotland against us, would be beaten entirely, as he had been at Gladsmuir or Prestonpans; and by the defeat of General Hawley he gained a considerable sum of money, and his honour was a little repaired. The Duke of Cumberland was immediately charged with the command of the army in Scotland. He left London on the 28th of January, and on the 30th he arrived at Edinburgh.

The destruction of our battery terminated immediately

the siege of the castle. The Prince, on the same day, learned the arrival of the Duke of Cumberland at Edinburgh, and made forthwith a review of his army at Bannockburn, with the intention of marching thither before him; but finding that he wanted a great many Highlanders, whom a long stay at Stirling, and the proximity of their own country, had tempted to return to their homes, to place their booty in concealment, our army was obliged to make a retreat to retain the mountainous districts, abandoning all our artillery to the enemy, with the exception of some field pieces, and, to our eternal shame, flying with precipitation before this same army which, sixteen days before, we had beaten hollow. How fortunate is an army when it has an able general at its head! One is led into these reflections when one thinks how the existence of thousands of men depends upon one man, whose error in judgment may render them in one instant unfortunate victims, by producing a numberless series of unfortunate events without remedy, the necessary consequences of a first error. The whim of being in possession of a paltry shed of a castle, without the possibility of its being of the least use to us, was the cause of a chain of events which made the Prince miscarry in his enterprise, and brought his partisans in great number to the scaffold. In a project vast and lofty, the greater part of men saw only part of it at a time, and very little of the whole with a general foresight of all the events which ought naturally to occur in the execution. The base of an operation being false, the erroneous consequences show themselves every day, and accumulate the one above the other.

We left Stirling on the 31st January to proceed to Inverness, a city the capital of the Highlands, thirty-four leagues to the north-west of Edinburgh; and having crossed the river Forth at the ford at Renfrew, our army passed the night at Crieff. The morning of our departing from Stirling the church of St. Ninians, where we had fifty barrels of powder, blew up with a terrible explosion, the conflagration having taken place by accident. The next morning, the 1st February, our army left Crieff in two columns, of which one, led by Lord George Murray, took the road along the sea coast, passing by the cities of Perth, Dundee, Montrose, *Peterhead*,* and *Aberdeen*, following always the coast; the other column, having the Prince at its head, crossed directly the mountains by Blair-Athole, which is by far the shortest road to Inverness. This column, with the Prince, having passed Ruthven in Badenoch, took there a fortress, also another about four or five leagues from that, called Fort Augustus, which King George had caused to be constructed to bridle the Highlanders and keep them in awe. These he immediately razed to the ground, and made the garrisons prisoners.

The Prince slept on the 16th at Moye, a castle of the Chief of the Mackintoshes, which is at the distance of two leagues from Inverness. Lord Loudon, Lieutenant-General in the service of King George, and Colonel of a Highland regiment, being at Inverness with about two thousand regular troops, the Prince wished to effect his junction with the other column before approaching nearer to that city. Lord Loudon formed the project of taking the Prince by surprise, who, nowise apprehending such an attack on his person, was in full security at Moye, and his Lordship was on the point of succeeding, but for that invisible power which pleases so often to manifest its sovereignty in over-turning the best laid projects of weak mortals. His Lordship, three hours after mid-day, caused a guard and chain of sentinels to be placed all around Inverness, as well inside as outside of that city, ordering them straitly not to allow any person to leave the town, under any pretext, or of whatsoever quality he might be. He commanded, at the same time, five hundred of his troops to hold themselves ready to march on the first order; and

---

* If they took Peterhead on their way, which is not at all probable, they must have passed Aberdeen first.—ED.

having assembled this body of troops without noise, and without alarming the inhabitants, he placed himself at their head and departed on the instant, regulating his march so as to arrive at Moye towards eleven o'clock at night.

The English officers having been drinking, at the house of Mrs. Bailly, tavern keeper at Inverness, waiting the hour of their departure, her daughter, who was about thirteen or fourteen years old, served them at table, and having listened attentively to their conversation, the little Bailly discovered their design, by the expressions which they let escape them. This generous child, at the moment that she was assured of the fact, left the house and escaped out of the town, in spite of the vigilance of the sentinels, and took directly the road to Moye, running with all her might, and having divested herself of her shoes and stockings, in order that she might run the faster to apprize the Prince of the danger with which he was threatened; and having accomplished these eight miles, always out of breath, she arrived at Moye before Lord Loudon; and the Prince, not doubting in any wise this surprise, had only time to save himself from the house of Moye in his dressing-gown, slippers, and night-cap, to conceal himself in the neighbouring mountains, where he passed the night. This dear child, to whom the prince was indebted for his life, was almost killed by the excessive fatigues of this race, but by the care which they bestowed upon her, she was recovered to life, and her health was quickly re-established.* The Prince, not being able to suspect an attempt so bold, had taken a very slender retinue with him to the castle of Moye.†

As soon as ever the little Bailly had raised the alarm, the Blacksmith of the village of Moye came to present himself to

* The people of Inverness ought to erect a monument to the little Bailly.—ED.

† This little episode is highly illustrative of the fine feelings of the female character, and a proof of the attachment and fidelity with which the Scottish peasantry, on every occasion, shielded the unfortunate Pretender, in all his dangers.—ED.

the Prince, to assure His Royal Highness that he had no occasion to leave the castle, that he would ensure for his head that he would cause Lord Loudon and his detachment return to Inverness more quickly than they had come. The Prince, from this, did not feel himself sufficiently secure not to seek his safety in flight to the neighbouring mountains. In the meantime the Blacksmith, for his own satisfaction, put his project into execution. He assembled promptly, a dozen of his comrades, and advanced with them, on the road to Inverness, until about a quarter of a league from the Castle; then he formed an ambuscade by placing six of his comrades at each side of the highway, to await there the arrival of the detachment of Lord Loudon, recommending to them not to fire till he should tell them, and not to fire all together, but one after another. When the head of the detachment of Lord Loudon was opposite the twelve men, towards eleven o'clock at night, the Blacksmith cried with a loud voice, "See these miserable villains who wish to carry off our Prince, fire my boys, don't spare them, no quarter!" He let fly, at the same time, shots of musketry on every side, and the detachment, seeing their project was discovered, all took to flight in the greatest disorder, imagining that this was our army which waited them; and they never stopped till at Inverness, dismayed and seized with the most terrific panic. Thus it was, that a simple Blacksmith, with twelve men, put to flight Lord Loudon, Lieutenant-General of the armies of England, with five hundred regular troops. At the first discharge of the Blacksmith, Lord Loudon had his fifer killed, who was at the head of the detachment, and they did not wait for a second.*

The Prince having next day assembled all his columns, which had passed the night in the hamlets at some miles

---

* The Blacksmith also deserves a memorial, his fertile genius equalling that of Hannibal, or any of the greatest commanders of antiquity. This recalls to memory the defeat of the Midianites by Gideon and his noble band of three hundred men, near the hill of Moreh in the valley.—*Judges*, Chap. vii. 19, 20, 21, 22.—Ed.

distance from Moye, advanced to Inverness, with a design of attacking Lord Loudon, and avenging himself of his attempt of the night before ; but his Lordship, on his approach to the town, retired, crossing the Frith, which is to the north of Inverness, after having collected together all the boats, barques, and other crafts which would have enabled us to pursue him ; and he carried them over with him to the other side of the Frith.

The citadel of Inverness was fortified according to the modern plan—a regular square with four bastions ; and its situation was advantageous, on an eminence which commanded the town. It was constructed in the time of Oliver Cromwell, and had always since been kept up, in order to hold subject to Government, the Highlanders, who are naturally brave, faithful, and generally attached to the House of Stuart. Since the Revolution in 1688, the maintenance of this fortress had cost the Government, as they pretend, more than fifty thousand pounds, sterling. The Commandant of the citadel, in a condition to sustain a siege, refused at first to surrender on the summons of the Prince ; but the trenches having opened, at the end of two days, he surrendered with his garrison, which consisted of two companies of Lord Loudon's regiment. The Prince immediately caused the fortifications to be razed to the ground, blowing up the bastions by mines. M. St. Epene, sergeant of the French cannoniers, who was charged with this operation, perished in it. This unfortunate man believing that the match had gone out, and having approached to examine it, the mine blew up, and tossed him in the air, with the stones, to an incredible height.

Our cavalry, which had taken the same road as the column of Lord George (Murray), arrived on the 16th at the river Spey ; a detachment passed that river at a ford, and stopped all night at Elgin, a town the capital of the province of Moray. On the 17th the column of Lord George came to Elgin, and on the 18th it advanced as far as Forres and Nairn, having served as an escort to the cargoes of two vessels which had arrived at Peterhead—one from France and the other from Spain, which consisted of money, arms, and ammunition. That from France had on board a piquet of the regiment of Fitz-James's cavalry. On the 19th the whole army joined at Inverness.

The English frigate, the *Hazard*, of about eighteen guns, which had been taken by the Highlanders in a singular manner, and sent to France to carry the news of our victory at Falkirk, was re-taken by the English on the 25th of March. Having been chased all the day of the 24th by the English ship-of-war the *Sheerness*, she ran ashore in Lord Ray's country, quite to the north of Scotland, where, having a hundred thousand crowns and other effects which she brought from France, the vassals of Lord Ray, who were attached to the House of Hanover, pillaged the cargo and made the crew prisoners, who had lost thirty-six men in the combat which she had sustained against the *Sheerness*, a ship of sixty guns. It was at Montrose the Highlanders had taken the *Hazard* without premeditated design. This vessel having been a-cruising for some time before that town, incommoded them much, firing continually when they saw any persons appearing on the shore, and being brought to anchor near the land, they galled the Highlanders greatly. One day it happened in a thick fog that they embarked in fishing boats, and the officers who were with them, having engaged them to approach little by little, as if by curiosity, for the purpose of examining a ship of war, one of which they had never seen before. As soon as the crew of the *Hazard* saw through the mist, the seamen, seized with a terrible panic, fell upon their knees on the deck and begged for quarter with clasped hands, terrified lest the Highlanders should attempt to come on board, and put them all to death at the point of the sword. The Highlanders immediately ascended on board, and took possession of the ship, but not being masters of navigation, they obliged their prisoners themselves to conduct it into the harbour of Montrose with a pistol at their throat. Intrepid men, animated and resolute, are capable of everything; but it is necessary also to have an officer of the same stamp at their head, capable of directing their operations, who knows their character, and what is suitable for them, not to sacrifice them by impossible enterprises, otherwise in place of prodigies, they would not prove but ordinary men. He who was at the head of the Highlanders, had the design of leaping on board and taking her by a *coup de main*, but he conducted them with finesse to its conclusion, without their perceiving his intention.

The Duke of Cumberland came to Stirling with his army on the 2nd of February. He stayed there till the 5th, the night of which he passed at Crieff, and on the 6th he arrived at Perth. He sent a detachment which seized the Duchess of Perth in her castle, because her son was with the Prince; also the Viscountess of Strathallan, who had her son and her husband in our army; and these two ladies were taken to the Castle of Edinburgh, where they were shut up in a narrow and unhealthy prison, and confined there for nearly a year. This trait of the Duke of Cumberland was unheard of and without example! To endeavour to make a mother answerable for the manner of thinking of her son, and a woman for that of her husband.

On the 8th of February the Prince of Hesse, son-in-law of King George, landed at Leith, the seaport of Edinburgh, with five thousand men and five hundred hussars, in the pay of England. He remained at Edinburgh till the 23d that he departed to go to Perth, with his troops in order to replace his brother-in-law, the Duke of Cumberland, who had gone to the north of Scotland with his army to come up with us. The Prince of Hesse, during his stay in Edinburgh, made himself beloved and esteemed by every one, by his moderate and upright conduct in presence of the partizans of the Prince, mixing indifferently in all societies, without appearing to take any personal interest in the quarrel between the Houses of Hanover and Stuart, and the Hessians, imitating the example of the Prince, conducted themselves in like manner.

The Duke of Cumberland sent a body of troops into the district of Athole—all whose men, vassals of the Duke of Athole, were in our army with Lord George Murray, his brother—and they there perpetrated abominable cruelties, burning the mansions of the gentlemen who were with the Prince; turning forth their wives and children in the midst of winter, without any shelter, to perish in the mountains of cold and hunger, and to which they added all sorts of infamies and horrors. When this was made known at Inverness, Lord George departed on the instant with the Athole men to take vengeance; and he conducted his march so well in passing by bye-paths across the mountains, that the enemy had no information of it. Having regulated his march so as to arrive at Athole at the beginning of the night, about ten o'clock in the evening, they all separated, dividing themselves into small detachments, and each gentleman taking the nearest road to his own house, where they surprised all the English in their sleep. Those who had thrown forth their families ready to perish with hunger and the inclemency of the season, and their wives and daughters violated by the brutality of these monsters, were not made prisoners; they were given up while they slept to the punishment which their inhumanity deserved. Thus they were all massacred or made prisoners, except two or three hundred men who had shut themselves up in the castle of the Duke of Athole, which Lord George could not force without artillery,—which it was impossible to transport across the mountains by the bye-paths, which it was necessary to take, to succeed in the enterprise. The Clan Athole was the most numerous in our army, about from twelve to fifteen hundred men.

The Prince of Hesse was then at Perth with his Hessian troops, at the distance of three or four leagues from the castle of the Duke of Athole at Blair. He learnt the news of this adventure. He sent immediately his Hessians to support the English, and oblige Lord George to raise the siege of the castle of his brother, of which he had formed the blockade. These Hessians having attacked Lord George, the Highlanders fell upon them with rapidity and impetuosity, sword in hand, and running after them quicker than their horses, they killed five or six Hessians, and made a Hessian Lieutenant prisoner. The next day Lord George sent this officer back with a letter to the Prince of Hesse, in which he demanded, in name of Prince Charles Edward, a cartel for the exchange of prisoners that they might make reciprocally; adding that if he would not agree to this, all the Hessians who had fallen into our hands, would at once be put to the sword. The Prince of Hesse communicated to the Duke of Cumberland the letter of Lord George Murray, representing this demand as just, but the Duke of Cumberland would not even choose to hear it spoken of. The Prince immediately declared to him that without a cartel, a single Hessian should not budge out of Perth; and he added that he had not sufficient interest in the quarrel between the Houses of Stuart and Hanover to butcher and sacrifice his subjects against these desperate people. So the Prince kept his word, having always remained at Perth with his Hessians, without choosing to go to the north of Scotland to join the English army, as the Duke of Cumberland wished him to do.

The Duke of Cumberland on his arrival at Aberdeen, a considerable town, distant about twelve leagues from Inverness, caused his army to be cantoned there to wait the fine season,* and the little town of Keith, in the district of Strath-

---

* While at Aberdeen, the Rev. John Bisset, one of the ministers of St. Nicholas Parish, and great grand-father of the Rev. Robert Fairweather of Nigg, acted as chaplain to the Duke; and that gentleman's other great grand-father, the Rev. John Angus, minister of Culsalmond, entertained him at his manse on his march to Culloden.—ED.

bogie, where he had some of his troops, was very near the centre of his cantonment. M. Glasgow, an Irish officer, in the service of France, proposed to the Prince to make himself master of their post at Keith, provided the Prince would only give him a detachment of two hundred men. The Prince hesitated at first to agree to it, having a great deal of mistrust of its success, but in the end consented to it. The enterprise of Glasgow was bold and hazardous; notwithstanding being conducted with prudence, and by an officer of experience, it succeeded to the full. He arrived at Keith at one o'clock in the morning, without its having been discovered, and according as he had regulated his march and calculated the time when it would be necessary for him to arrive there. To the " Qui va la? "—(Who goes there?) of the sentinel before their body guard, M. Glasgow replied " a friend," and advanced himself to the sentinel whom he killed with a stroke of his dagger, and the Highlanders, on the instant, rushed upon the guard, who at first made some resistance, but they were all soon disarmed. Then, without loss of time, the Highlanders ran through the town to make the soldiers prisoners, who were lodged in the houses of the inhabitants; and M. Glasgow conducted himself so well, that in less than an hour, he accomplished his operation, and retired with four hundred and twenty prisoners, whom he presented next day to the Prince. This grand exploit had a good effect, and made such an impression upon the English, that not believing themselves longer in safety in any part, they were obliged to redouble their posts in the middle of winter, in a mountainous country, excessively cold, the fatigues of which brought upon them so much disease that the hospitals at Aberdeen, the head-quarters of the Duke of Cumberland, were continually full of soldiers.

Lord Loudon, with his corps, tormented us, and frequently gave us uneasiness. He sent out detachments which crossed over the Frith, always giving us alarms, and when we wished to attack them they re-embarked and re-crossed immediately to the other side—not being able to pursue them for want of boats, we were obliged to suffer the insults with patience. This position of Lord Loudon became the more unpleasant to us, on our being assured that the Duke of Cumberland waited only the good weather to attack us; for Lord London would be able to pass the Frith when we were ourselves engaged with the English army, and place us between two fires. Thus it was of the last importance to find out the means of being able to attack Lord Loudon and disperse his detachment.

The Prince caused all the ships, barques, and fishing boats which they could find at Speymouth, and in the other small ports on our side of the Frith, which appeared to be about a league in breadth, to be brought to Findhorn; and on the night of the 19th or 20th of March, they there embarked as many men as they were capable of holding, under the orders of Perth, who commanded this expedition. The Duke departed with about eighteen hundred men, and there happened unexpectedly in the morning a thick mist, very favourable to the enterprise, under cover of which the Duke conducted his whole detachment close to the enemy, without their perceiving him, until the Highlanders were at no greater distance from them than about fifty paces, and then they saw them advancing at a quick pace, sword in hand. The enemy was so confounded at seeing them so close upon them, ready to fall upon them, that the greater part of them threw down their arms to the ground, and surrendered prisoners. Some few saved themselves by flight, of which Lord Loudon was one of the number. The Duke of Perth returned the same day to Inverness, with many hundred prisoners, without having fired a single musket shot, or shed a single drop of blood.

On the 19th, after that, the detachment was commanded by the Duke of Perth, M. Macdonald of Scothouse came to pass the day with me. He was a man of about forty years of age, endowed with a fine figure and a prepossessing address, joined to that an agreeable exterior. He had all the qualities of soul which ordinarily distinguish the honourable and gallant man—brave, polite, obliging, of fine spirit and sound judgement. Although I had not known him but since the commencement of the expedition of the Prince, I soon came to distinguish his merit and the sweetness of his society. I formed with him the closest friendship, notwithstanding the disparity of our ages. He paid back my affection with all the tenderness of a parent. As he was naturally of a gay disposition, I perceived his melancholy on his entering my dwelling. On asking him the cause, this worthy man looked at me, his eyes bathed in tears—"Ah, my friend, you do not know what it is to be a father. I am of this detachment which must depart this evening to attack Lord Loudon. You do not know that a son whom I adore is with him an officer in his regiment. I believed myself fortunate in obtaining that rank for this dear boy, not being able to foresee the descent of Prince Charles Edward into Scotland. Perhaps to-morrow I shall have the grief to kill my son with my own hand, and that the same ball that I shall fire off in my defence may occasion from myself a death the most cruel! In going with the detachment I may be able to save his life; if I do not march, some other may kill him." The recital of poor Scothouse rent my heart. I could not refrain from mingling my tears with his, although I had never seen this young man, the subject of the sharp pangs of a tender father. I retained him the whole day at my house, endeavouring to dissipate his fears as much as I possibly could, and making him promise on parting to come straight to my house on leaving the boat. The next day, at evening, I heard a great knock at my door. I ran thither, and perceived the good father holding a young man by the hand, of a jolly figure, who cried to me, his eyes sparkling with joy. "Behold, my friend, the one who yesterday caused all my alarms. I have taken him prisoner myself; and when I had hold of him he embraced me fervently, not regarding the others who were present." I then saw him shed tears of joy, very different from those of the night before. We supped all three together at my chamber, and I never had my mind more penetrated with satisfaction than at this supper, by the mutual scene of tenderness between the father and the son.*

M. Cameron of Lochiel departed, on the 18th of March, with his men, for the purpose of going into his own country, and having taken M. Grant with him, and some pieces of cannon which we had found in the citadel of Inverness on its reduction, in order to besiege Fort-William in his country, which greatly harassed his vassals. He commenced the siege of this fortress on the 20th, which only lasted a few days. This was the last of these forts in the Highland districts which remained to be taken by us. They razed it immediately to the ground, as they had done the others. Having made more English soldiers prisoners, since the commencement of our expedition, than we had of Highlanders in our army, it was an extreme embarrassment to be able to guard them—above all, our moving army being always on the march, they escaped continually, and in the end very few of them remained with us; but what was more provoking, they rejoined their different regiments, and we had always those same soldiers to fight with, whom we had already vanquished, and those whose lives we had spared; a considerable advantage to the English, to get back again by thousands, soldiers whom they had no right to count upon. We had two ways of avoiding this inconvenience. To send them into France; this was not so easy to be done, owing to the difficulty of finding ships to transport them; indeed, not to make prisoners at all, by putting them all to the sword, an equal law, as we were certain to perish on the scaffold, as

* This little episode between father and son exhibits a fine feeling of tenderness, very pleasing to contemplate, and equally creditable to both. —Ed.

many Scotchmen as might be made prisoners. This last course is too cruel for persons who think humanely, as we had done, although just; and this was the kind of war we ought to have followed, to have inspired properly with terror the enemy, and not to have continually the same men to fight with. Besides, the English soldiers, at one time dispersed, would not have sought with eagerness to join their standards as they had done before,—nor to expose themselves *a second time*, by *deserting*, to the swords of the Highlanders, knowing that they would receive no quarter; but they perceived our goodness even to weakness, and that they ran no farther risk than to be made prisoners again, with life in safety.

Mr. Peter Smith, of whom I have spoken already, who had always most singular ideas, proposed to the Prince a middle course, which was to cut off the thumbs of their right hands, in order to put it out of their power to hold their muskets. The over-weaning affection of the Prince for the English nation, the uprooters of his House, always hindered him from adopting any advice which could give them displeasure.*

We had four to five hundred English officers prisoners, to whom the Prince gave permission to retire where they might judge proper, after having granted their parole of honour not to serve against him during the space of eighteen months. Those who were made prisoners at Falkirk, the Prince made add at Stirling their oath to their parole of honour, in order to bind them more firmly. But the Duke of Cumberland, on leaving Edinburgh, sent circular letters to all the English officers, our prisoners, to absolve them from their parole of honour, and declaring, that they could not be bound to keep their parole of honour with rebels; and he added,

---

* It is said, that on one occasion, Cæsar was guilty of a similar cruelty, by causing the hands of a certain tribe, who had made a desperate resistance and committed great depredations, to be cut off; a statement hard to be believed in one, who in general, showed such kindness and humanity towards his enemies.—ED.

that, if they did not immediately rejoin their different regiments, he would punish their disobedience by bestowing their
commissions on others. To the eternal disgrace of the English
officers, there were not but four who refused to accept the
absolution of the Duke of Cumberland. They were the
Chevalier Halket, Lieutenant-Colonel of the regiment of
Lee, taken at the battle of Gladsmuir or Prestonpans; and
M. Ross, son of Lord Ross; with two other officers, who
replied to him,—"That he was master of their places, but
not of their honour and probity." *

News reached Inverness that the Duke of Cumberland,
having collected his army, had left Aberdeen the 8th of April,
to come up with us, and that he had taken the road by Banff
and Oldmeldrum. The Prince immediately sent Lord John
Drummond to Elgin with his regiment of Royal Scotch, five
piquets of the Irish brigade, Lord Elcho with our cavalry,
and a piquet of the regiment of Fitz-James, newly landed at
Peterhead without their horses, but with their saddles, bridles,
and other cavalry accoutrements; and he had them mounted
in haste, for good or bad. Lord John was ordered to scour
the banks of the Spey, and to dispute with the Duke of Cumberland the passage at the fords of that river. The Prince
relying on the resistance of Lord John in there making all the
obstacles possible to defend the fords, and imagining that if
Lord John should not be able altogether to render it impracticable, at first by fortifying it by good intrenchments, he
would retard the advance of the Duke of Cumberland; so as
to give him time to reassemble his whole army,—of which
almost the half had returned to their homes with their Chiefs,

* Similar to this, but of a more impressive nature, was the reply of
Viscount Darte to the order of Charles IX., to massacre the Huguenots of
Bayonne—"Sir, among the inhabitants of this town and your Majesty's
troops, I could only find honest citizens and brave soldiers, but not one exe-
cutioner; we jointly, therefore, beseech your Majesty to command our arms
and lives in things that are practicable." This great and generous soul
looked upon a base action as a thing impossible.—*Montesquieu*—ED.

in order to revisit their families, and to put all their vassals in a state to carry arms, without exception. Besides the excessive scarcity of provisions at Inverness, was moreover a further motive to allow them to depart, the Prince assuring himself that they would rejoin his army with diligence and alacrity, the moment they were ordered to return. One may imagine how every one was confounded at Inverness, on learning, like a clap of thunder, that the Duke of Cumberland had passed the river Spey, at the fords, without there finding the least opposition. There was nobody but Lord Elcho—who had always served with the greatest distinction—at the fords, with his troop of guards, who fired a few musket shots at the English during the time they were in the river; but they were immediately forced to wheel round, and with great difficulty were able to make their retreat, assaulted on every side by the English cavalry, who pursued them vigorously.*

Lord John Drummond had remained at Elgin with the body of infantry which he commanded, the distance of two leagues from the ford, without having made the smallest disposition to defend the passage of the river. Mr. Hunter, of Burnside, an officer of the troop of guards, escaped narrowly being made prisoner. Firing his pistol at the enemy, he wounded, most unfortunately, his horse in the neck, which threw him to the ground, but at the moment that the English were ready to seize him, he jumped on a horse, behind a guardsman, and both saved themselves. The little knowledge of Lord John Drummond in the art of war, appeared to us so much the more extraordinary that he was a General officer

* The coming of Lord John Drummond into Scotland was the cause of all the disasters that befell the Prince. It occasioned his retreat from Derby at a time when he could have gone triumphantly to London; and the six guns which he brought with him from France, deprived the Prince of the fruits of his splendid victory at Falkirk. His supineness in not opposing the passage of the Duke of Cumberland at the river Spey, is unintelligible and admits of no excuse.—ED.

in the service of France. It is incomprehensible that persons of illustrious houses, destined by their birth to command armies, to occupy the first offices, and to enjoy the first ranks in the kingdom, do not attach themselves with liking and assiduous application to the study of the military art, in order to enable them to discharge their duties with honour and distinction to the advantage of their king and country; so much the more, that the shame and dishonour,—the necessary consequences of military blunders, which ignorance in the art of war exposes them to make continually,—are never to be effaced, and cover them with infamy during their whole lives. The little efforts which they make to acquire it, is a proof of the small estimation in which they hold it.*

In proportion as the army of the Duke of Cumberland advanced, all our posts fell back to Inverness. The Prince sent to advertise all the Chiefs absent on leave, to return there with diligence. He had the disagreeableness of learning that M. the Earl of Cromarty, with his son Lord Macleod, having been surprised in the Castle of the Countess of Sutherland by a detachment commanded by M. Mackay, in the service of King George, had been made prisoner, and carried immediately on board a ship of war, *The Hound*, to be transported to London. This deprived the Prince of the Clan of the Mackenzies, of about five or six hundred men.

For some time provisions had become very scarce at Inverness; our army suffered severely, and it was badly nourished. There was no longer money in our military chest, the Prince not possessing, on the whole, more than five hundred Louis d'or; and without any means of obtaining any

* "Man," says M. Thomas, "has need to learn even the most simple things. He is condemned to drawl on in separating one truth from another. Could there then be an art so much complicated as that of navigation, which one can apply equally to the military art in general? It would require an ignorance sufficiently daring for one to flatter himself that he could succeed in it without having studied it. Nature gives talents—power confers titles—study alone gives knowledge."—*Elege de Rene du guay Trouiner*, 1761, p. 47.

in the Highland districts, where we were precipitated blindly, by the extreme indigence of the inhabitants. Our communication with the low country being completely cut off by the English army, shut up as it were in the mountains, everybody experienced the misery more or less. The richer landlords of our army were so embarrassed as to be unable to defray their own expenses; labourers could not extract money from their farmers.

The Prince caused our army leave Inverness on the 13th of April, in order to occupy a position which he had chosen for a field of battle, at a distance of half a league from that city; and we remained there night and day, lying on the ground under the clear sky, without tents or shelter against the inclemency of the weather; the Highlanders having nothing for food but some biscuits and cold water. I kept myself with my friend Scothouse, who parted with me the little victuals which he could get hold of, and giving me equally during the nights, which were very cold, the half of his bed-coverings, and a share of the straw which he had made the Highlanders of his regiment collect. On the 15th of April, the birth-day of the Duke of Cumberland, the Prince judging that this fete would be celebrated by the English, even to daylight, formed the project of surprising the Duke of Cumberland in the following night, and attacking him in his camp at Nairn, distant from three to four leagues from the entrance in front of the castle of Culloden, where we had stopped since the 13th. For this purpose he made our army at once to defile without noise, towards eight o'clock at night, marching by two columns, of which Lord George Murray—as was generally the case—was at the head of the first, which acted as guide to the second, which the Prince conducted himself. This march, across the fields, in a dark night without being able to follow a road, had the inevitable result of all night marches, being attended with disorder and confusion, and was most painful. The Highlanders not being able to keep themselves together by the difficulties of the bad roads, scattered themselves more or less, and there were a great many laggers. Besides there being many bad passes to clear in the obscurity of the night, it would have been impossible for the best disciplined troops in such a situation to preserve order. Lord George at the head of the first column, when he was at the distance of a quarter of a league from the English camp, at the entrance of a meadow which extended as far as their camp, made his column halt, and sent to inform the Prince that it was absolutely necessary to wait there a little to form the Highlanders into battle array, according as they should come up, in order to form a front and attack the enemy together, and in order. This advice of Lord George was much approved of by M. Hepburn of Keith, and by M. Cameron of Lochiel, who were both with him at the head of the first column, and who always appeared to me very sensible and reasonable; but the Prince—who did not see the necessity of stopping to form themselves into battle array, and attacking altogether, in place of making it helter-skelter and scattered—sent back an aide-de-camp with orders to Lord George constantly to advance and attack the camp of the Duke of Cumberland immediately, and that he would come up in such manner as he was able. Lord George, on this answer from the Prince, in place of continuing to advance to the English camp, took immediately a road upon his left, retracing his steps. He said to M. Hepburn that it was too late, that the day would appear before he could arrive at the camp of the Duke of Cumberland, and the surprise being discovered, the enemy would be able to profit by attacking us while in disorder and dispersed. M. Hepburn answered him that it would not be a great evil as it would require but little daylight to enable the Highlanders see to lay about their sword strokes; but Lord George would not hear him, and remained inflexible in his resolution of returning to the Castle of Culloden upon the instant, without attempting anything.

The Prince not knowing of the retreat of Lord George, and imagining the first column to be always before him, longed to fall upon the camp of the enemy; but as soon as he perceived his mistake, he made a complete face about, and our army arrived at Culloden about seven o'clock in the morning, everybody being wearied and fatigued, and in despair at not having accomplished anything.

I never could comprehend the idea of the Prince wishing to attack the English army, so superior in number to his own, with even only a part of his own force in disorder, without waiting till the whole force came up, and without getting them formed into battle array, to present a front of attack— without which could we fail to be repulsed shamefully? It is necessary that a surprise should be not only concerted with exactitude and foresight of all the consequences naturally expected to occur on the part of the enemy, but be conducted and supported at the same time with sagacity by all the means possible to render it successful. In fact, an enemy surprised is half vanquished; it is not the same if he have time to recover himself; he can soon find resources for escaping you, or perhaps destroying you.

I do not pretend to justify the false step taken by Lord George in retreating with the first column, contrary to the orders of the Prince, and without advertising him of it. Stopping at the entrance of the meadow to await the arrival of the whole force, scattered by the obscurity of the night in bad roads, he could have insisted with the Prince on the absolute necessity of forming themselves in battle array, in order to attack the enemy according to.the opinion of people of sense, and to convince him of the absurdity of acting otherwise. The Irish, people of contracted notions, whom the Prince had adopted solely as his counsellors in everything, made by their clandestine whispers Lord George to be suspected of treason in this manœuvre; but knowing him better than any one, I could not attribute his disobedience of the orders of the Prince but to his violent and ungovernable character. Exhausted by hunger, and overwhelmed with the excessive fatigue of the three last nights, as soon as we had returned to Culloden I galloped to Inverness at full speed, where, wearied to repair my strength by sleep, I undressed myself almost asleep, and having already one leg in bed, ready to stretch myself between two blankets, what a surprise! At that moment I heard the drum and trumpets of Fitz-James sounding "To horse, to horse"! which struck me like a clap of thunder. I put on my clothes again, my eyes half shut, and mounting my horse I returned back on the instant to our army, *(a.)* upon a rising ground, *(c.c.)* where we had remained for three days, and from which we saw the English army, distant from us about two miles. They seemed at first inclined to encamp there, many of their tents being already pitched; but all of a sudden the tents disappeared, and we saw them immediately in motion to advance towards us. The sight of our army making preparations to give battle, to appearance, made the Duke of Cumberland change his design; and he would have committed an extreme mistake to defer attacking us forthwith, in the miserable condition in which our army were, overcome and reduced with hunger and fatigue; perceiving, above all, by our manœuvre of our impatience to give battle, with all the disadvantages possible, and that we were well disposed of ourselves to advance to our own destruction. The Duke of Cumberland was ignorant till day of the danger to which he had been exposed during the night, and as soon as he learned it he decamped and followed close upon us.

The Prince, on his return to Culloden, furious against Lord George, said in presence of every one that no person but himself in future should command his army; * but as soon as

* If Prince Edward had done nothing else but sleep all the time of his expedition, and left Lord George Murray to act, according to all appearance, he would have found, on awakening, the Crown of England on his head.

the English army began to appear, they represented to the
Prince, always ardent and forward to give battle without
looking at the consequences, that the Highlanders, overpowered with fatigue, dispersed and lying in profound sleep
in the cottages and in the enclosures in the neighbourhood,
it was impossible that he could then bring them forward to
the combat, on account of the difficulty of finding them.
Besides, what could be hoped for from people in their situation; overcome for want of sleep and nourishment, and
altogether cut up by this night's march—a thousand times
worse than all those they had ever gone through in England,
and which they ought not to ascribe to supernatural power.*
They advised him to retire to the eminence, *(g.)* his left
supported by the ruins of the castle, *(b.)* where he could
place advantageously his cannon in batteries, occupying at
the same time the town of Inverness, and leave his army
to refresh themselves and take sleep; that with twenty-four
hours' rest, he would find them re-established and altogether
different men. It is certain that in this advantageous position, by raising an intrenchment *(l.l.l.l.)* to cover the town
of Inverness, we would have had nothing to fear from the
Duke of Cumberland coming to attack us all at once, if he
examined narrowly our position; and if he had done so, he
would have paid dearly for his rashness. Thus we could
have calculated to remain there quietly for some days; above
all, the delay would have given time for all those absent on
leave to return to the army. But the Prince would hear
nobody, and he must give battle, at whatever price it was to
be bought.†

* Men are like quadrupeds. One may be able to push them to a certain
point, but not to overwhelm them. Pass that degree, they fall supine
under the weight, and become useless.

† There is nothing more true than what Herodotus says:—" I imagine
that it is a great advantage to consult well with regard to affairs before
undertaking their execution; at least, if events are sometimes contrary to
wise deliberations, one has always this satisfaction of mind, that he has

The ground on the bottom, between the Castle of Culloden *(f.)* and the enclosure *(c.)* upon our right, was marshy,
and the water mid-way up the leg—well chosen for affording
us a protection from the English cavalry. The English were
drawn up in battle order, in three lines; and we had difficulty
in forming two, the second of which was composed of the
Irish piquets, with the regiments of Royal Scotch of Kilmarnock, Lord Lewis Gordon, the Duke of Perth, Lord Ogilvie,
Glenbucket, and of John Roy Stuart, the two last of which,
and that of Lord Kilmarnock, had but small force—about
two or three hundred men per regiment. When the English
army had approached to the height of the enclosure, *(c.)*
distant about three or four hundred yards from the eminence,
(e.) our army then descended into the marshy deep, and
advanced, running, to charge the enemy, sword in hand.
The Prince having remained at the entrance of the eminence
with the piquet of Fitz-James's, beyond the shot of the
enemy's musketry, he saw the English engaged in breaking
down the walls of the enclosure *(a.)* to take us in flank, and
he sent immediately order upon order to Lord George Murray
to throw a force into the enclosure, during the time that his
lordship was at the head of the first line, ready to fall upon
the enemy, in order to prevent that manœuvre of the English,
which could not fail to prove fatal to us; but Lord George
paid no attention to it, and the English having accomplished
the breaking down of the wall of this enclosure, there entered
it two regiments of their cavalry, with four pieces of cannon,
which they got to play upon our right with grape shot, close
to the muzzles, producing a fire so terrible that they mowed
down our right wing, like as they cut down a field of corn,

followed good counsels, and that it is nought but chance that has triumphed over prudence. But when one has followed evil counsels, and
fortune has favoured them, truly he has succeeded in his design, but likewise he has this disgrace, that he owed his success, only to chance and
fortune."

and swept away whole ranks. By the unevenness of the
marshy ground, our right and the centre were the first to
come in contact with the enemy; our first line making some-
what of an oblique, but overwhelmed by a fire so terrible in
flank, our right were unable to sustain it, and were obliged
at once to take to flight, while our centre had already pierced
the first line of the enemy, and cut through the second; and
the left, where I was with Scothouse, was not more than
twenty paces from the enemy, who let fly their discharge at
the moment when the right began to be on the retreat, and
which communicated itself from the right to the left of our
army with the quickness of a flash of lightning. What a
moment of horror! To see these same Highlanders who
advanced to the enemy with the boldness of lions, and with
resolute countenances, in an instant flying like timid and
terrified cowards. Behold the instability of man! One
might say that the attack of the Highlanders resembled
greatly that of the French, which is a violent flash, the fire
of which is more ardent than durable. Troops, howsoever
powerful they may be, have not the unflinching qualities
which render them invincible.

It was evident that the English being in possession of the
enclosure, our destruction became the natural consequence.
The Prince saw this perfectly from the eminence *(a.)* where
he was, and he sent an aide-de-camp as many as six or seven
times, with orders to Lord George Murray to take possession
of that enclosure; he perceived that he did not obey these orders,
but he did not quit his place upon the eminence. It was in
the meantime a critical moment, when it was necessary that
he should show the heart of a dragoon in advancing at once to
put himself at the head of his army, and directing himself the
manœuvres which he wished it to execute. He never would
have experienced any disobedience on the part of his subjects, who had offered their lives a sacrifice to re-establish
him upon the throne of his ancestors, and who would have
shed for him even the last drop of their blood.

There are occasions when it is necessary for a General to expose his person, and not to remain beyond the reach of musketry; and there never was a necessity more real than this for exposing himself to some musket shots, since the gain or the loss of the battle depended upon it. In the desperate expedition he had undertaken he ought to have faced all dangers, without seeking too much either to live or die, conducting himself with bravery and prudence, and following circumstances as they occured. But he was surrounded by some Irishmen, his confidants, in whom the baseness of their souls corresponded with the lowness of their birth. Besides that nation, remarkable in England for having their judgment perverted in their ideas, were not in general but very bad counsellors. But the Prince allowed himself to be blindly led by their advice. The Prince fought for a crown, and in consequence was the one of all his army most interested to succeed; on the other hand, the Scotch had no other recompense in view but to escape from the effects of their rashness, in so much exposing themselves voluntarily to death upon the scaffold, with confiscation of their estates.

As far as I could distinguish, at the distance of twenty paces, the English would have appeared to me to have formed six ranks; the three first ranks kneeling on the ground, they discharged a running fire the most terrible. My unfortunate friend, Scothouse, was killed by my side, without my being so sensibly affected at the moment that I saw him fall, as I have always been since. It appears to me that the Power who presides in battles over the lives of men, cuts off those who have the greatest merit, and spares the most unworthy. The soldiers, who are susceptible of friendship, are those to be deplored. The fatal lot of my friends has often cost me tears, and left, moreover, an impression on my mind of pain and regret which can never be effaced. M. Macdonald of Keppoch, absent on leave with his Clan, having made the greatest diligence in his march to join the Prince, and having arrived at the moment of the charge, had time to take his place in the first line, but was killed immediately. He was a worthy man, of rare merit, who had the regrets of every one.

Our defeat did not surprise me, on account of the overwhelming state of the Highlanders, ready to succumb from fatigue, hunger, and want of sleep; but I was astonished that in their situation they comported themselves so well.* If our right had only been able to resist three minutes more, the English army, which was violently and rudely shaken, would have been repulsed by the shock of our right wing, which was no more than the distance of five-and-twenty paces from the enemy, when the rout of the right began; and if our centre had been supported which had pierced the enemy's first line, it is not doubtful but that the English would have been immediately put to flight. There was about twelve hundred men killed on the field of battle, and of that number there was as many of the enemy as of the Highlanders, so that our loss was not considerable.†

* Suntse, the Chinese General, has said,—"In unfurling your standards, obtain for yourself the first regards of your soldiers; be attentive to their actions, and by their ardour or indifference calculate on good or bad success. It is not a more deceitful omen than that of the first bearing of an army ready to engage in combat. It is so much so, that having promised the most signal victory, it would have been entirely defeated, if the battle had taken place a day sooner or some hours later." I believe there would have been few in our army, except Prince Edward, who could have expected to gain this battle in the deplorable state of the Highlanders, and who would not have wished to postpone till next day giving battle, to afford them time to refresh themselves, to sleep, and to eat.

† "It is not," says the celebrated Montesquieu, "the actual loss which one makes in a battle, (that is to say of some thousands of men), which is fatal to a state, but the imaginary loss, and the discouragement which deprives it of the self-same forces, as if fortune had left it."—*Considerations on the Rise and Fall of the Romans*, page 39.

It is inconceivable in theory, that two armies which regard one another as of equal force should come to encounter each other, losing an equal number of men, and that which is repulsed in an instant not looking upon itself more like an equal part, although their loss is the same, dispersing and allowing themselves to fall in pieces in the confusion of detail, without daring successfully to make head against his enemy, of which the equality between the two armies continues to be the same as before the attack.

SUPPOSED THE

BATTLE FIELD

OF

CULLODEN,

BUT NO TITLE GIVEN

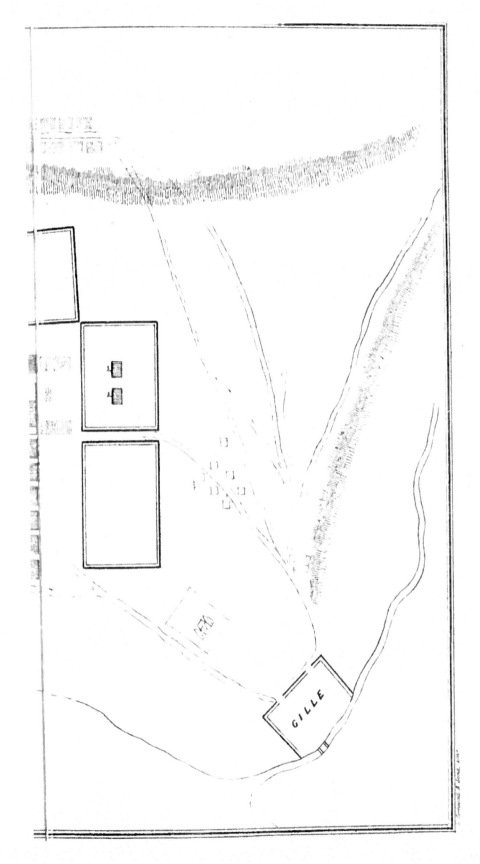

The right of our army threw itself upon the bank of the river Nairn, and encountered in their way a corps of English cavalry, which found themselves as much embarrassed as the Highlanders; but the English Commander, acting most wisely, opened through his centre to offer them a passage, and allow them to defile at the distance of pistol shot without molesting them or seeking to make any prisoners. There was but one English officer of the corps who attempted to make a Highlander prisoner, and advanced some steps before to seize him, but the Highlandman dealing him a blow with his sabre killed him; and not content with that, he stopped himself sufficient time to enable him to strip him of his watch, and then decamped with his booty. The English Commander, tranquil spectator of this scene, renewed his instruction, that no persons should leave their ranks, and could not refrain himself from laughing, and rejoicing that this Highlander had been able to escape on account of his boldness, without appearing to deplore the fate of his brother officer who had disobeyed his orders. If this corps of cavalry had not acted thus prudently, they would have been in a moment cut to pieces. It is extraordinarily dangerous in these routs to endeavour to cut off fugitives from the means of saving themselves. Our left, which threw themselves towards the side of Inverness, were much more ill treated, having been pursued by the English cavalry. The road from Culloden to Inverness was all along strewed with the dead. The Duke of Cumberland had the cruelty to leave the wounded among the dead upon the field of battle, despoiled of their clothes, from Tuesday, the day of our miserable battle, till Friday, three hours after mid-day, when he sent detachments to kill all those whom they should find alive; and there were many of them who were struck down by their arms, after having resisted for a time the continual blows. He caused set fire to a barn where there were many of our unfortunate wounded Highlanders, and having surrounded it with troops, soldiers, with their bayonets fixed to the mouth of their muskets, drove back into the flames those unfortunate men who attempted to save themselves, burning them inhumanly, as if they had not been of the human race. This sanguinary Duke was obliged to have an act of the English Parliament to indemnify him for these actions, with many others of the same kind, which he perpetrated, contrary to the laws of the realm of Great Britain. His cruelties showed a soul cowardly and ferocious.

The Prince, when he saw the rout commence, saved himself with some cavalry of the piquet of Fitz-James. Lord Elcho found him some hours after the battle, in a hut near the river Nairn, surrounded by Irishmen, not a single Scotchman being with him. He was in total prostration, lost to all hope of being able to retrieve his affairs, having his mind completely imbued with the evil counsels of Sherridan and other Irishmen, who governed him at their will, and giving up every design but that of saving himself in France as soon as he possibly could. Lord Elcho represented to him that this defeat was nothing in reality, and his Lordship did all in his power to persuade him to dream of nothing but to rally his army, put himself at their head, and try once more his fortune. This disaster, he said, could be very easily repaired; but the Prince was insensible to all his lordship could say, and would not hear him.

I arrived, on the 18th of April, 1746, at Ruthven, which by a mere chance happened to be the rendezvous for rallying our army, without its being pointed out. I found there the Duke of Athole, Lord George Murray, his brother; the Duke of Perth, Lord John Drummond, his brother; Lord Ogilvie, and a great many other Chiefs of Clans, with about four or five thousand Highlanders, all in the best disposition possible for renewing the contest, and having their revenge. Ruthven is a small village, distant about eight leagues from Inverness, by a road across the mountains, very narrow, full of precipices, and where there are many defiles where one hundred men could defend the passages against ten thousand, solely by rolling* down rocks from the summit of the mountains.†Lord George Murray sent at once a force to defend these defiles; at the same time he despatched an aide-de-camp to inform the Prince that a great part of his army was collected

* " Nature has spread throughout the whole universe," says a celebrated author, "objects worthy of our contemplation; and when she ceases to deprive us of these boons, she attracts more our regards even by the terror she inspires us with; but amid the horrors with which she sometimes envelopes herself, and which ought to enter into her treasures to compose the system, whence results the universal good, nothing merits more the attention of an intelligent and curious being than these enormous masses of rock, and these precipices in the mountains of Scotland, from which one could not look below into these vast abysses without trembling and having the sight confused."

† The situation of the mountains of Scotland seems to resemble greatly the description of the Alps in the narrative of the passage of Hannibal into Italy. The pathways at the sides of the mountains, of about two feet in breadth, where, if one should make a false step, one would tumble down frightful precipices three or four hundred feet deep; and the tops of these mountains might be from three to four hundred feet in height above the footpaths, and bristling points quite through the enormous rocks, where the mountains would form a shelter to descend or fall upon the footpaths; but there would be no need of this. By rolling stones from the summits upon the enemy engaged in the defiles, they would be able to stop the passage of an army of a hundred thousand men. Besides, in these places there are many little valleys commanded and overhung by the mountains all around, very sharp, where there were only two gorges, one for entering the valley and the other for leaving it, resembling exactly that of Thrasymene. The Duke of Cumberland was a furious character, rash, impetuous, and headstrong. He would have attempted, without doubt, to force us in these mountains; and he could not have failed to have had his army cut in pieces, as were the Romans at Thrasymene. Hannibal had fifty thousand infantry and nine thousand cavalry. According to Polybius, his army was reduced on the passage of the Alps to twenty thousand infantry and six thousand cavalry opposed to the barbarians. The Duke of Cumberland had to make head against these Highlanders, who had gained many victories in the open plain against the English armies composed of the best troops, and double the number of the Highland army. Prince Edward did not see the infinite advantages of such a place. Lord George Murray knew them, and would have availed himself properly of them, if the Prince had not sent the order to Ruthven to disperse.

together at Ruthven; that the Highlanders were armed, full
of ardour, and breathing with impatience for the moment to
be led back to the enemy; that the Clan Grant, and other
Clans of Highlanders who had until then remained neuter,
were disposed to declare themselves for him, seeing the
destruction of their country inevitable by the proximity of
the victorious army of the Duke of Cumberland; that all the
absent Clans would return thither in a few days, and that in
place of five or six thousand men who were present at the
Battle of Culloden, as well by the absence of these into their
own country on leave, as by those who had dispersed themselves on arriving at Culloden on the morning of the 16th
for the purpose of going to sleep, he could reckon at least on
eight or nine thousand men, even more than he had ever had
in his army. Every one beseeched the Prince most earnestly
to come thither quickly to put himself at their head.

The day of the 19th passed at Ruthven without there
being any news of the Prince. All the Highlanders were in
an astonishing joy and ecstacy, such as no one had ever
before seen in a beaten army, hoping with impatience every
moment to see the Prince. But on the 20th the aide-de-
camp, whom Lord George had sent to him, arrived to an-
nounce to us as all the answer on the part of the Prince—
" that every one should look out for the means of saving
himself as he best could "—a reply not a little dispiriting and
heart-rending to those brave men who had sacrificed themselves for him.* We were masters of the defiles between
Ruthven and Inverness, which would have given us time to

---

* Some critic who might be in our situation might say the Prince ought to
have despaired of nothing; it is on occasions when everything is to be feared
that nothing ought to be feared. It is when one is surrounded with all
dangers that he ought to fear none. Lo! what are we to think of a Prince
who made his *debut* with an audacious rashness, landing in Scotland with
only seven men. With the best combinations a man may fail in his enterprises, but the fortitude he shows in his misfortunes gives a splendour to
his virtues and resources.

re-assemble our army; the Clans of the MacPhersons of Cluny, of five hundred brave men, also a great many more Highlanders who had not been able to return to Inverness before the battle, came to rejoin us at Ruthven, in so much that our number increased at every moment; and I am convinced that in eight days we should have had an army stronger than ever, capable at once of re-establishing our affairs, and promptly avenging the horrors and barbarities of the Duke of Cumberland. But the Prince was unalterable, and immovable in his resolution to abandon the enterprise, and terminate most ingloriously his expedition, the rapid progress of which had attracted the attention of all Europe. He had nobody about him but the Chevalier Sherridan and other Irishmen, who were altogether ignorant of the situation of the country and the character of the Highlanders, and who had nothing to lose, but on the contrary, much to gain, in proceeding to France, where many had already commenced to lay the foundations of their fortunes. The breaking up of the entire force at Ruthven produced a most touching and affecting scene. There were eternal adieus when they took leave of one another, no one being able to forsee his fate, or that his days might not be ended on the scaffold. The Highlanders sent forth screams and howlings, groaning and weeping with bitter tears at seeing their country at the mercy of the Duke of Cumberland, on the point of being ravaged, and themselves and their families reduced to bondage, and plunged in misery without remedy.

An accident, which took place at Inverness some days after the battle, would have been very advantageous to us if the Prince had joined us at Ruthven. A young gentleman, named Forbes, a relation of Lord Forbes, a cadet in an English regiment, having quitted his colours to join himself to the Prince, had the misfortune to be made prisoner, and was hanged at Inverness, indiscriminately with other deserters, without any distinction. While the corpse of Forbes hung upon the gibbet, an English officer, brutal and beastly, plunged his sword into the body of Forbes, with an oath that all his countrymen were as great traitors and rebels as he was. A Scotch officer, who happened to hear the impertinence of this Englishman, took his sword immediately in his hand, and demanded the reason of the insult which he had offered to his country; and while they were fighting with one another, all the officers took part in the quarrel, in so much that swords were soon seen to be drawn on every side. The soldiers at the same time, of their own accord, sounded the bugle, took up arms, formed a line along the streets, the Scotch on the one side and the English on the other, commencing a very spirited bayonet fight at the musket points. The Duke of Cumberland being out of town, they advised him forthwith, and he returned with the utmost speed, before this revolt had made great progress. He addressed himself immediately to the Scotch of his own army, and soothed their minds by his praises, telling them that all the times he had had the honour of commanding them, he had always found their fidelity and attachment to his House, as well as their bravery and their good conduct; and in the end he appeased them.

Thus it was that Prince (Charles) Edward commenced his adventure with seven men, and abandoned it at the moment when he could have been at the head of more than seven thousand — preferring to run into the mountains all alone, exposed to be taken and poinarded at every instant by the detachments of English troops which the Duke of Cumberland had sent after him, and who followed in his track, often passing quite close to him, whose pursuit he escaped as if by a miracle—rather than put himself at the head of a body of brave men, of whose fidelity and attachment he was assured, and who would fight to the last man in his defence. This had become their sole resource for saving themselves from the scaffold, for the preservation of their firesides, for preventing their families from being outraged by furious, barbarous, and

insolent soldiers, and preventing the ruin and destruction of
their country, which it was impossible to hinder from being
devastated, by an enemy ready to enter it, finding it without
defence ;—besides, a country bristling with precipices, with
defiles half-way up the mountains where no more than one
man could pass at a time without being able to be turned,
offered all the chances of defending themselves, were there a
thousand men against ten thousand, for years ; and there
could be no want of food, as long as there was great abun-
dance of horned cattle, since their riches consisted of these, of
which they sold a hundred thousand annually to the English ;
but this war of chance was only our last resource, for I was
always morally persuaded that in eight or ten days we should
have been in a state of returning to Inverness, and of fighting
the army of the Duke of Cumberland on equal ground.
Every time that I think of it, I am constantly surprised that
Lord George Murray and the other Chiefs of Clans did not see
it advisable to sustain this war of the mountains themselves in
their own defence.* That would have saved much blood,
which was shed in the end on the scaffolds in England, have
prevented the almost total extermination of the Scotch Highlanders, which was effected afterwards by the policy of the
Government, whether it was by the transportation of their

---

* There is nothing more true than that which a celebrated author says—
"That when people raise the standard of revolt, in taking the sword it is
necessary to throw away the scabbard—there is no middle course : it is necessary either to conquer or perish." It was thus that Crœsus counselled
Cyrus to repress the Lydians after their revolt at Sardis : "But, in order,"
said he, "that they may not have any more cause to give you trouble and
to rise against you, cause them to have for their defence arms in their houses,
order them to carry a mantle above their dress, to put off their buskins ;
moreover, order that they instruct their children to play on instruments of
music, to sing, to drink : thus you will immediately find men converted into
women, and there will be no more reason in future for you to fear that they
will revolt against you." "Crœsus gave this advice to Cyrus because he
imagined that this condition was more favourable to the Lydians than to be
reduced to slavery and miserably sold."—*Herodotus*, vol. ii., page 136.

families to the Colonies, or by the number of Highland Regiments which they had raised, and which were many times
almost annihilated and renewed during this last war. When
one sees brave troops well disposed, it is necessary to take
advantage of their ardour; and it is a great talent of a General to know the occasions, and distinguish when they are
favourable.*

Prince Edward, during some months, was pursued with
eagerness by detachments of English troops, and so closely
that scarcely had he left a hiding place ere they arrived at
it; sometimes, even, he was surrounded on every side. The
Duke of Cumberland never failed to say to the Commandants
of these detachments, the moment of their departure, "Make
no prisoners—you understand me." It was in their particular
instructions to stab the Prince, if he fell into their hands.
But the Divine Wisdom frustrated the atrocious and barbarous resolutions and designs of this sanguinary Duke; the
officers of whose detachments, his executioners, committed
more cruelties upon the brave but unfortunate Highlanders
than could have been done by the most ferocious savages of
Canada. The generous, noble, and heroic action of Mr. Ro-
derick Mackenzie contributed greatly to save the Prince from
these assassins thirsting for his blood.

Mr. Mackenzie, a gentleman of good Scotch family, had
served during the whole expedition of the Prince in his Life
Guards : he was in the suite of the Prince, and resembled
him a little for those who were not accustomed to see them
together. Mackenzie was in a hut with the Prince and two
or three other persons, when all at once they were told that
they were surrounded by detachments of English troops, who

---

* The English, following the maxim of the Cardinal Ximines in regard to
the Moors, that the only way of preventing them from raising themselves
was to place them in an absolute inability to do so. They disarmed the
Highlanders, forbidding them henceforward to carry arms ; at the same
time, by an Act of Parliament, they obliged them to change the form of their
costume, which was the ancient dress of the Romans, and to wear trowsers.

debouched from every side, as if they had been informed posi-tively that the Prince was in the hut. The Prince at this moment was asleep, and they awoke him to apprize him of his dismal state—that it was morally impossible for him to be able to save himself. He replied, " It behoves us then to die like brave men, sword in hand." " Not so, my Prince," said Mackenzie to him, " there is yet another resource. I will assume your name, and I will go before one of the de-tachments. I know what will be my fate; but while I am engaging them your Royal Highness will have time to escape." Mackenzie rushed like a fury, sword in hand, upon a detach-ment of fifty men. In falling, covered with wounds, he said to them, " You don't know what you have done; I am your Prince, whom you have slain "—in saying which he expired immediately. They chopped off his head, which they carried instantly to the Duke of Cumberland, nobody doubting that it was not that of Prince Edward; and this barbarous Duke, yielding to his wishes in believing himself to be in possession of the head of the Prince, departed next day for London, with this head packed up in his post-chaise.

The depositions of many persons at London, who affirmed that it was the head of Prince Edward, had a good effect in rendering less vigilant and active the English troops in their pursuit, which, hitherto, had formed a chain all the way from Inverary to Inverness; and the Prince saved himself, many times at very great risk, having been obliged to traverse this chain between their detachments. M. Morison, his valet-de-chambre, was then in prison at Carlisle, condemned to death. The Government sent there a Messenger of State, to suspend the execution of the sentence, and to conduct M. Morison to London, in order to get him to declare, under solemn oath, if it was the head of Prince Edward. But M. Morison having been attacked by the way with a most violent fever, with transports and delirium, was confined to bed in the house of the Messenger, where they guarded him during five days after his arrival in London ; and when he began to recover, the head was then in such a decomposed state, that they deemed it useless to examine him upon it, not being able to distinguish a single feature. They granted M. Morison his pardon ; and he went at once to France, where he is still living.

In the end, Prince Edward embarked on the 17th of September (O.S.), in a ship which M. Welsh, shipowner at Nantes, had expedited and sent into Scotland, in the Highland districts, expressly to search for and save him ; and he landed at Marlaix, in Brittany, in the month of October, after having escaped a thousand times perishing by the poinard, and having been exposed during five months at every instant to the loss of life—encountering a thousand times more dangers than he would have done in his Expedition with courage and firmness, at the head of his faithful Highlanders, while he had reason to hope to be able to make head against the English, and to reserve for the last resource that of concealing himself and running among the hills, without attendants, till the defiles should have been forced, and till he had no other means of forming a force to oppose the enemy.

But our situation was not desperate ; and all that one can say is, that this Prince had undertaken his Expedition with rashness, without reflecting, and without foreseeing the personal dangers to which he would be exposed : he had continued it throughout in the same manner, always sparing his person from the risk of musket shots ; and in the end threw it to the winds, at a moment when he had a thousand times more cause to hope for its success than when he had left Paris to undertake it.*

* We may, perhaps, conclude this Volume, not inappropriately, by an anecdote of Her present Majesty, applicable to the House of Stuart. One day Her Majesty came into the Library, and inquired at the Librarian what progress he was making with the Stuart Papers—adding, with much *naivete*, "You must know, Mr. ———, I am a devoted supporter of the House of Stuart." "Madame, your Majesty will pardon me," was the ready reply, "if I say that I am an equally devoted supporter of the House of Hanover."—ED.

ImTheStory.com

Personalized Classic Books in many genre's

Unique gift for kids, partners, friends, colleagues

Customize:

- Character Names
- Upload your own front/back cover images (optional)
- Inscribe a personal message/dedication on the
  inside page (optional)

Customize many titles Including
- Alice in Wonderland
- Romeo and Juliet
- The Wizard of Oz
- A Christmas Carol
- Dracula
- Dr. Jekyll & Mr. Hyde
- And more...

Lightning Source UK Ltd.
Milton Keynes UK
UKOW05f0921221016

285899UK00014B/385/P